NONVIOLENT RESISTANCE

A New Approach to Violent and Self-Destructive Children

This book begins with an examination of Gandhi's "nonviolent" resistance and its application to the family context. A model of escalation processes between parents and children is presented, as well as ways for overcoming escalation. The book includes a step-by-step instruction manual for parents. Special topics include: dealing with violence against siblings, dealing with children who take control of the house, building alliances between parents and teachers, and community uses of approach.

Haim Omer is Professor of Psychology at Tel Aviv University.

NONVIOLENT RESISTANCE

A New Approach to Violent and
Self-Destructive Children

HAIM OMER
Tel Aviv University

Translated from the Hebrew by
SHOSHANNAH LONDON-SAPIR
AND HAIM OMER

CAMBRIDGE
UNIVERSITY PRESS

PUBLISHED BY THE PRESS SYNDICATE OF THE UNIVERSITY OF CAMBRIDGE
The Pitt Building, Trumpington Street, Cambridge, United Kingdom

CAMBRIDGE UNIVERSITY PRESS
The Edinburgh Building, Cambridge CB2 2RU, UK
40 West 20th Street, New York, NY 10011-4211, USA
477 Williamstown Road, Port Melbourne, VIC 3207, Australia
Ruiz de Alarcón 13, 28014 Madrid, Spain
Dock House, The Waterfront, Cape Town 8001, South Africa

http://www.cambridge.org

First published 2004

Printed in the United States of America

Typefaces Stone Serif 9.5/14.5 pt. *and* ITC Symbol   *System* LaTeX 2_ε [TB]

A catalog record for this book is available from the British Library.

Library of Congress Cataloging in Publication Data

Omer, Haim.
    Nonviolent resistance : a new approach to violent and self-destructive children / by Haim
Omer ; translated from the Hebrew by Shoshannah London-Sapir and Haim Omer.
        p.   cm.
    Includes bibliographical references and index.
    ISBN 0-521-82948-8 – ISBN 0-521-53623-5 (pb.)
        1. Children and violence.   2. Violence in children – Prevention.   3. Child rearing.
4. Passive resistance.   I. Title.

HQ784.V55O45   2003
649′.1 – dc22   2003055283

ISBN 0 521 82948 8 hardback
ISBN 0 521 53623 5 paperback

This book is dedicated to my son Noam,
who gave me the first push.

CONTENTS

FOREWORD

The multitude of values, approaches, and opinions in modern society renders it helpless to confront the violent and self-destructive acts of children and teenagers. Confusion and conflict of opinion between parents or even between the same parent's different positions lead to bewilderment and paralysis. Professionals, be they educators, therapists, or community workers, are no more of one mind than are parents. In this book I try to show there is a way out of the stalemate. The answer comes not from one psychological theory or another but from a political-social approach: the doctrine of nonviolent resistance. This doctrine, the philosophical and ideological roots of which are ancient, evolved into a practical, detailed, and consistent theory following the work of Mahatma Gandhi. In his struggle against the discrimination against the colored in South Africa, against religious and class violence in India, and against the British occupation, Gandhi demonstrated the power of nonviolent resistance and its amazing ability to mobilize supporters, to impassion activists, to empower the weak, and to curb violence and oppression. The singularity of this doctrine resides not only in its high moral standards, but also in its success in preventing escalation, which is probably the thorniest problem for any approach that attempts to deal with violent or otherwise extreme behaviors.

The novelty in this book is its translation and application of the doctrine of nonviolent resistance to violent and self-destructive children and adolescents. I argue that nonviolent resistance allows parents, teachers, and therapists to find a common denominator and create a joint front, where previously there was a chaos of conflicting views and mutual accusations. The doctrine's unifying and mobilizing value has been proven among hundreds of parents, who previously had no notion that a clear, determined, and nonviolent approach was available. Parents and teachers who were helpless, isolated, defeated, and insecure succeeded in recovering their confidence, self-esteem, and stature in the face of the extreme behaviors of children.

This book includes a step-by-step instruction manual for parents on how to implement nonviolent resistance (Chapter 3). The practice-oriented reader might begin by perusing this manual, with the advantage that the opening chapters on the principles of nonviolent resistance and on escalation processes will then make more immediate and concrete sense. The instruction manual is actually an independent feature of the book: parents who begin implementing the program may show it to those who are willing to support them in their endeavor. This is one of the ways in which we used the manual in our research project at Tel Aviv University: copies were handed out both to the parents and to their potential helpers (friends and relatives).

I want to thank my student Bella Levin for her help in evolving a graphic presentation of the escalation model. I want to thank the therapists in my project at Tel Aviv University (Uri Weinblatt and Carmelit Avraham-Krehwinkel), the students who offered the parents support, and all the parents who struggled heroically and nonviolently in recovering their own parental presence and in curbing their children's violent and self-damaging acts.

NONVIOLENT RESISTANCE

A New Approach to Violent and Self-Destructive Children

1 NONVIOLENT RESISTANCE: A NEW APPROACH TO VIOLENT AND SELF-DESTRUCTIVE CHILDREN

Parents and professionals face a dilemma when dealing with children's violent and self-destructive[1] behaviors. The behavior of these children is characterized by lack of boundaries, uncontainable outbursts, and an ever growing readiness to go to extremes. Most of these children are deeply averse to being supervised or guided by their parents or by other responsible adults. When a confrontation arises, they usually convey the message: "Leave me alone!" or "I am the boss!" The parents of these children inevitably find out that their usual ways of reacting, or those suggested by professionals, are ineffectual. When they try the way of reprimands, threats, and punishments, the child responds in kind, escalating the aggressive behaviors. When they opt for the way of persuasion, acceptance, and understanding, the child often not only ignores these gestures, but also reacts with contempt. The home, which should be a safe haven for the family, becomes then a battlefield where the slightest disagreement may turn into a violent clash. No wonder that, sooner or later, the parents become exhausted and opt for submission, which at least promises a temporary quiet.

This quiet, however, proves illusory. It soon becomes apparent that parental submission leads to an increase in the child's demands. The relationship then gets caught in a vicious circle: **parental submission → growing demands by the child → growing parental**

---

[1] I term "self-destructive" those behaviors that put the child's safety and development at a high risk. For example: school absenteeism, drug abuse, delinquent activities, and sexual promiscuity.

frustration and hostility → **retaliation by the child** → **parental submission**, and so forth.

The failure of the "tough" and the "soft" parental approaches leads to two kinds of escalation: complementary (in which submission increases demands) and reciprocal (in which hostility engenders hostility). Complementary escalation is asymmetrical and is characterized by the dynamics of blackmail. In this process, the more extreme the child's behavior, the more the parent is inclined to buy quiet by concessions. The message the child gets is that the parent is too weak to stand up against his[2] threats. The child thus becomes used to getting what he wants by force, and the parent, to submitting (Patterson, Dishion, & Bank 1984).

Reciprocal escalation is characterized by a mutual rise in hostility. In such interactions, each side feels that the other is the aggressor and that one is acting only in self-defense. The highest levels of hostility are reached as a result of this sense of being trapped (Orford 1986). In parent-child relationships, this happens, for instance, when the parents try to impose authority by force or when they react to the child's aggressiveness in kind (threatening, cursing, shouting, hitting). The two sides may then get caught in a spiral of growing violence.

In addition to their peculiar damaging effects, both types of escalation fuel one another. Thus, as the parents submit, they gradually become more frustrated and angry, approaching their boiling point. Studies show that the more helpless the parents, the greater the risk of their losing control (e.g., Bugental, Blue, & Cruzcosa 1989). Conversely, the more violent the mutual outbursts, the more frightening they become, until the parents reach the point where they are ready to submit. The parental pendulum thus swings continuously between giving in and hitting back. We are thus faced by a paradox: supporters of the gentle way are liable to be provoked to violent outbursts, and supporters of the tough way are liable to flee in panic to submissiveness.

---

[2] To avoid sexist language, I alternate between masculine and feminine pronouns.

This pendular escalating motion is one of the central problems in parents' dealings with children's violent and self-destructive behaviors. Its damages are far-reaching: (1) the child becomes more and more power-oriented, while the parents become more and more helpless; (2) the parents learn to ignore the child's negative behaviors in order to avoid confrontations; this response becomes habitual, so that the parents eventually stop noticing many of the child's negative behaviors; (3) the relations between parents and child grow ever more negative and narrow; and (4) the child feels the need to back her power by bouts of extreme behavior.

This brings us to the chief question of this book: How can we act so as to effectively counter reciprocal and complementary escalation at once? The answer, as we saw, must be different from either the "gentle" or the "tough" way. The way we propose is that of *nonviolent resistance*.

Nonviolent resistance is a doctrine that was developed in the sphere of social-political struggle. Groups that have fallen victim to oppression evolved it as a means of defending themselves and effecting change. There are various reasons for choosing nonviolent resistance: a moral reluctance against using violence, an awareness that the other side is at an advantage in the use of strong-arm methods, the understanding that verbal persuasion is ineffective and that nonviolent methods will lead to fewer injuries and losses than violent ones. These reasons are also valid in the family context. Many parents recoil from violence on moral grounds, fear its damaging consequences, and understand that when it comes to naked force, the aggressive child is far less inhibited than they. Parents also frequently experience the failure of verbal persuasion. Parents have, in addition, one very special reason for choosing nonviolent resistance: their love for the child. As we see below, nonviolent resistance is the form of resistance that best expresses parental concern and love.

In this chapter, we present the basic principles of nonviolent resistance, basing ourselves on the doctrine and life-work of its chief exponents (especially Gandhi) and on the analyses of Gene Sharp (1973), the main theorist and historian of this approach. We also indicate how each principle and method is applicable to the family framework. The translation of the principles into concrete steps is presented in the instruction manual for parents in Chapter 3.

A few words on terminology: We use the terms "power," "control," "oppression," and "dominance" as if they were relevant for the behavior and goals of the aggressive child. The reader might object that the aim of violence in the socio-political sphere is power, whereas the aggressive child's behavior is probably motivated by wholly different psychological needs. But is this really the case? Unlike the child who expresses anger as a result of some fleeting frustration or strain, the aggressive child develops systematic behaviors whose apparent purpose is to preserve her total freedom of action, attain benefits, minimize competition, and frighten the parents into helplessness. In this situation, the goals of the aggressive child resemble the objectives of violence in social and political contexts, that is, the attainment of maximum power with minimum interference. In many cases, the parents' occasional attempts to curtail the child's total independence and power by, for instance, increasing his or her supervision may lead to severe retaliation. This has given professionals justification for referring to these parents as "victims of abuse" (Cotrell 2001). In this respect, the situation of the aggressive child's siblings is frequently even more precarious than that of the parents (Finkelhor and Dziuba-Leatherman 1994; Loeber & Stouthamer-Loeber 1986). We would therefore assert that the more the behavior of the child aims at frightening and paralyzing the parents, and the worse the parents' and siblings' suffering, the more shall we be justified in using the terminology of "power," "oppression," "control," and "dominance" and in recommending the use of nonviolent resistance.

NONVIOLENT RESISTANCE IS A WAY OF FIGHTING

One must not confuse nonviolent resistance with a position that views all use of power as invalid. Gandhi, the most uncompromising ideologist of nonviolence, emphasized time and again that socio-political conflicts are decided by power. Demands or entreaties that are not backed by the power to resist have no influence (Sharp 1960). The language of nonviolent resistance is thus explicitly a language of struggle. According to the doctrine of nonviolent resistance, a person who desists on principle from fighting ultimately contributes to the perpetuation of violent oppression.

Leaders such as Gandhi and Martin Luther King, Jr., define "violence" in a specific and tangible way: a violent act is an act that is directed toward physically damaging the opponent (killing, wounding, destroying infrastructures) or emotionally damaging him by insults or humiliation (derogatory labeling, explicit provocation, rude gestures). The nonviolent activists abjure violence in this tangible sense. This definition of violence, however, does not include actions whose purpose is to disrupt the activities of the violent side, but do not inflict physical or verbal harm. On the contrary, these actions are precisely the ones that characterize the stance of the activists as *resistance*.

The definition of violence that we suggest in coping with violent and self-destructive children is similar: one must desist from any physical attack or counterattack, from any expression whose aim is to humiliate or insult, and from any deliberate provocation. In addition, parents and teachers must identify actions that lead to escalation and discontinue them. Examples of such actions are arbitrary punishments, threats, and shouting matches. The objective of nonviolent resistance is to restore the standing of parents and educators in a decided but nonviolent and nonescalating manner, even in the face of the child's harshest behaviors.

Following in the footsteps of the foremost exponents of nonviolent resistance, we talk openly about the parents' fight against the child's extreme behaviors. In evolving the readiness to fight, the parents must also become willing to call the child's behavior by name. Terms such as "violence," "abuse," and "exploitation" should not be avoided or prettified. In the following brief example, the opposite tendency is illustrated, in which an attempt was made to speak as euphemistically as possible about the harsh situation at home.

The mother of a twelve-year-old boy requested help as follows: "My son has a problem: when he feels the need to express himself, the expression tends to transfer to the physical plane." When the therapist asked for clarification, she added embarrassedly: "Something causes him to begin to activate his arms and legs." The therapist requested further clarification. The mother explained that her son kicked her and hit her with his fists. To the question what she did to stop the violence, she replied: "The question is what he has inside him that causes him to behave like that!"

The probable underlying assumption of the mother in this case is that understanding and empathy are the keys to solving the problem. The counterassumption of nonviolent resistance is that empathy and understanding, as essential as they may be, cannot take the place of a clear stance that violence must be defined as such and decidedly resisted. An empathic attitude does not suspend the parents' obligation to ensure that they, the child, and others will not be harmed. As we see below, the willingness to fight violence with nonviolent means not only does not prevent an empathic, understanding, and respectful attitude toward the child but actually creates the basic conditions for this attitude.

Viewing nonviolent resistance as a fight clarifies the connection between this concept and the concept of "parental presence." As I made clear in my book *Parental Presence: Reclaiming a Leadership Role in Bringing Up our Children* (Omer 2000), parental presence becomes manifest when the parent acts in ways that convey the message: "I'm here! I am your parent and will remain your parent! I am not giving in to you or giving up on you!" Parental presence is many-faceted: the parent is present as the child's guardian, educator, and companion. The parent is also present as an individual in her own right. How does nonviolent resistance relate to all this? *Nonviolent resistance is the fighting side of parental presence.* This means that from all the aspects of parental presence, nonviolent resistance is the one that becomes manifest in the parents' struggle against the child's destructive behaviors. As we see below, although nonviolent resistance is the fighting side of parental presence, it also enables the parent to become present in other ways in the child's life.

NONVIOLENT RESISTANCE AS OPPOSED TO VERBAL PERSUASION

The alternatives to nonviolent resistance are violent conflict and verbal persuasion. Nonviolent resistance is opposed to violent conflict in its decided avoidance of violence; it is opposed to verbal persuasion, in its understanding of the need for a real fight. For example: demanding higher wages by means of explanations and arguments would be the choice of verbal persuasion; sabotaging machines or occupying a factory by force would be the choice of violent struggle; staging demonstrations, strikes, and obstructive sit-ins would be the choice of nonviolent resistance. The same distinctions hold for the parent-child relationship. Thus, the tough or violent parent is the one who has recourse to threats, screams, humiliation, physical coercion, and physical or otherwise extreme punishments; the soft parent is the one who adheres solely to persuasion, entreaties, rational arguments, and expressions of empathy and affection; the parent who opts for non-violent resistance is the one who is willing to resort to such means as coming in person to the places where the child engages in self-destructive behaviors, sitting in protest in the child's room until she comes up with a solution to stop the violence, withholding services to the child that are extorted by threats, mobilizing the "public opinion" of friends and relatives against the child's violence, establishing an extensive supportive net to help search for the child when she evades parental supervision or runs away from home, and evolving with teachers and community workers a common front against antisocial norms.

As opposed to persuasion, the lever of nonviolent resistance is not verbal exchange. On the contrary, nonviolent resistance begins where words stop being effective. Opting for nonviolent resistance means acting so that the perpetuation of oppression and violence is gradually made impossible. Verbal exchanges precede nonviolent resistance and accompany it all along but do not replace it. All the exponents of nonviolent resistance believed that explanations, arguments, and entreaties that are not grounded on the spiritual and material strength of the resisting side convey a message of surrender.

The paradoxical phenomenon that verbal arguments, entreaties, and explanations may achieve the opposite of what was intended is well known to the parents of aggressive children. The more the parents talk, the more the child is convinced that they are not prepared to act. Parental verbalization then works as a guarantee that the child can continue to do as she pleases. For this reason, many children, particularly adolescents, try to involve parents in arguments. They know from experience that when the parents argue they do not act. Parents sometimes describe their children as "lawyers." These "lawyers" know for a fact that so long as the parents continue talking, they will forgo action.

Parental verbalization is also harmful in that it supplies the fuel for escalation: the parents' requests turn into demands and their demands into threats. The child repays in kind: arguments are met with louder arguments and threats with harsher counterthreats. Sometimes escalation frightens the parents into a return to soft requests. This transition, however, also results in escalation, but of a complementary kind: the child then reacts to the parents' softening with contempt and increased demands. This negative cycle is interrupted when the parents turn to nonviolent resistance, because they then learn not to be drawn into escalating verbalizations.

As in the socio-political sphere, the transition to nonviolent resistance in the family gradually arouses nonviolent reactions in the child. In face of the failure of violence to achieve its aims and in face of the determined nonviolent resistance of parents and teachers, the child begins to respond positively. We call this process "identification with the nonaggressor." In our opinion, it is no less common than the "identification with the aggressor" so familiar from psychology books.

NONVIOLENT RESISTANCE IN THE FACE OF VIOLENCE

In opting for nonviolent resistance, we must not assume that the opponent will desist from violence. On the contrary, we must expect that she will use all the means at her disposal, especially those that have proven effective in the past. However, in the face of our decision to respond to violence with nonviolent resistance, violent steps become problematical, inefficient, and self-limiting. The efficacy of nonviolent resistance against violence is based on an *asymmetry of means*: the more the violent actions of the other side are met with a determined nonviolent opposition, the more rapidly will they wear themselves out. This process was called by Sharp (1973) "the jiu-jitsu of nonviolent resistance." Violence is robbed of its strength for various reasons: (1) it loses its sense of legitimacy; (2) it undergoes inhibition by the opponents' nonviolent stance (it is much harder to attack people who sit quietly than people who swing fists and shout threats); (3) its perpetrators' confidence is shaken by the message of endurance conveyed by nonviolence; and (4) the asymmetry causes third parties to support the nonviolent side. Gandhi compared the condition of violence in the face of nonviolence with that of a person who hits the water with all her might: the arm is bound to tire before the water does (Sharp 1973). In this manner nonviolent resistance abrogates the conditions that perpetuate violence and creates an environment in which violence finds it hard to survive.

For these reasons, the violent side often tries to provoke the nonviolent side into violence. Success in this tactic would provide the violent side with new fuel. Correspondence from the era of British rule in India during the nonviolent struggle for independence reveals that the British authorities fervently wished the Indians to go back to violence, for they knew how to deal with violent acts (Sharp 1973). The history of nonviolent resistance is filled with incidents in which the rulers attempted to infiltrate agents into the nonviolent camp, in order to stage or instigate violence.

In the family sphere, it is common for aggressive children to attempt to provoke their parents to lose control and return to their "normal" outbursts. The aggressive child knows full well how to deal with a raging parent but is at a loss when confronted with a determined stance of nonviolent resistance. The preparation of parents to withstand such provocations is essential for any program of nonviolent resistance.

A divorced father who received custody of his twelve-year-old son had difficulty getting him up in the morning to go to school. The father initiated a program of sit-ins to get the child to go to school. After the first sit-in, the child did get up in the morning, but lingered a long time over breakfast. The father, who had to leave for work, tried to hurry him to finish the meal. The boy answered that the father had not requested nicely enough. The father asked him again politely. The boy commented that the "magic word" was missing. The father said the word "please." The boy went to his room and when the father entered a few minutes later, he found him sitting by the switched-off computer pretending to type on the keyboard. The father, who had not been properly prepared by us, lost his self-control and dragged the child to school by force. An hour later, the boy ran away from school, disappeared for the rest of the day, and told his mother and the school counselor that his father had hit him.

EMERGING FROM ISOLATION AND THE NEED FOR OPENNESS

The isolated, oppressed individual is subject to demoralization, fear, and weakness. The situation changes completely when the individual emerges from isolation. Many have marveled at the courage of nonviolent activists in the face of extreme repressive measures. Gandhi stressed that this courage is born not out of the isolated person's soul but out of the experience of togetherness. The very dialogue that makes victims' aware that the oppression is arbitrary is also a result of togetherness. The emergence from isolation also helps to give publicity to the injustices, thus enabling support from third parties who are not directly involved in the struggle. This, in turn, increases the sense of justice and the power of endurance of the activists.

To tap sources of support, nonviolent resistance must implement a policy of openness. For this reason, movements of nonviolent resistance operate in ways that are diametrically opposed to those of underground organizations: in place of secrecy, nonviolent resistance opts for candor and publicity. On a practical level, opting for openness may be far from simple. For example, as long as the movement is in its infancy, keeping it secret may be necessary for survival, for arrest of its leadership might lead to its obliteration. On the other hand, secrecy counters the central strategy of nonviolent resistance, which is based on wide support and on appeals to public opinion. Gandhi added another reason for opting unconditionally for openness: secretiveness stems from fear and is bound to perpetuate fear. Thus, instead of helping overcome paralysis, the habits engendered by secrecy actually deepen it.

These arguments also hold true for the relations between parents and children. For parents to successfully make the transition to nonviolent resistance, they must be encouraged to break out of isolation and secrecy. Attempts to preserve secrecy and avoid the inclusion of others weaken the parents and help sustain the child's violent behavior. A basic rule about family violence is that *secrecy perpetuates victimization*. Therefore, enlisting the support of relatives, friends, and community workers is an essential step in the transition to nonviolent resistance. "Public opinion" also plays a role in domestic violence. For example, friends and relatives can be asked to let the child know (personally, by phone, by letter, or by e-mail) that they are aware of her violent behavior and support the parents in their efforts to stop it. These manifestations of "public opinion" have considerable influence on children.

Breaking the seal of secrecy may be difficult for parents for two reasons: they feel a sense of shame regarding their good name and they want to avoid damaging the child's standing and future prospects. Therapists should express respect for these parental attitudes, while clarifying the crucial importance of emerging from isolation. The parents are of course given the right to decide who will be let in on the secret and to what degree. However, the principle remains that as long as the parents avoid including others, they will stay weak. One may also make it clear to the parents that the secret is bound to come out: incidents such as running away from home, suspension from school, or arrest cannot remain hidden. Parents soon realize that the very act of revelation changes the picture: paralysis and fear are reduced, the child gets a message of parental determination, and the options for coping with threats and violence increase. Breaking out of secrecy and emerging from isolation is often a "turning of the tables" that more than anything else undermines the power of violence.

The parents of a fourteen-year-old girl came to counseling when they found that their daughter was offering sexual services to children at school and through the Internet. The girl had even printed a visiting card indicating her willingness to engage in unconventional sexual practices. The parents feared that any confrontation would lead to extreme reactions. Their fear that the girl might run away from home or have recourse to prostitution paralyzed them. The therapist suggested coopting a number of family members and friends to convey to the girl a clear message of support for the parents and to help them search for her when she disappeared. At this point, a difference between the father and mother became manifest: the father was prepared to involve some of his relatives and friends, whereas the mother felt that shame prevented her from telling anybody what was going on in the family. The therapist clarified to the mother that the girl would interpret her refusal to involve anybody else as a sign that only the father was ready to fight. The mother was gradually convinced to bring one of her relatives to the next therapy session. The father saw her agreement as a very significant support.

Understanding that the courage to act grows out of supportive contacts may prevent a common therapeutic mistake. Many therapists view the lack of readiness to take action, for instance, in a battered wife or an abused mother, as a sign of lacking motivation for change.

This therapeutic attitude often leads to a breach in the alliance with the client. The position of nonviolent resistance is quite the opposite: in meeting with isolated parents (or other isolated victims), we first of all ask what support can be enlisted in their favor. To this end, the resources of the extended family, friends, and community agencies should be examined in detail. In our program, we also offer the parents help in addressing these potential helpers and in explaining to them the principles of nonviolent resistance, which have great mobilizing power and considerably increase the readiness to help. We then witness that as support becomes available, the parents' willingness to take action grows apace. This method constitutes a sharp departure from the usual approach to the problem of "lack of motivation." Instead of waiting until the willingness to act matures from within, or of futilely attempting to "pump up" motivation for change, therapists following nonviolent resistance act to reduce the client's isolation. In this manner, many parents who had formerly seemed chronically unmotivated were found capable of a very determined nonviolent fight.

Many parents would rather keep their resistance plans or even the fact they are in therapy secret from the child. They believe that openness would allow the child to cover her traces or go to greater extremes, so as to deter them. This secretive attitude is foreign to the spirit of nonviolent resistance. The attempts of the child to cover her traces are a small price to pay for the parents' recovery of their right and ability to openly supervise her doings. Parents must not become detectives who shadow their children in the dark but should openly reassert their presence in their lives. By choosing openness, parents are also manifesting the desired asymmetry of means: the child with violent or antisocial leanings is the one who is liable to opt for lies and camouflage, while the parents opt for openness and directness.

The mother of a sixteen-year-old boy who used to come home late at night asked me whether she should shadow him so as find out what he was doing and with whom he was involved. I suggested instead that she announce to him that she was not prepared to go on living in ignorance of his whereabouts and in passive acceptance of his late returns. If he came home after the agreed time, she would make phone calls and meet with people until she could ascertain where, how, and with whom he was spending the late hours of the night.

BREAKING AUTOMATIC OBEDIENCE AND THE MONOLITH OF POWER

Nonviolent resistance in the social arena is born out of the understanding that the oppressor cannot perpetuate his rule unless the ruled accept it as inevitable. The ruler will accordingly try to prevent the subjects from evolving this understanding, by keeping them in a state of automatic obedience and in the belief that the existent order is god-given and self-evident. Conversely, breaking automatic obedience and becoming aware that authority is arbitrary will undermine the hold of the ruler.

These phenomena are well known in the sphere of domestic violence. It is well known that violent husbands try to keep their wives in a state of unquestioning obedience. As we have repeatedly observed, violent children often relate similarly to their parents and siblings. Thus any sign of independence or disobedience by the victims may arouse sharp reactions by the violent child, so as to erase any notion that disobedience is possible. One of the chief aims of nonviolent resistance is therefore to break the parents' habit of automatic obedience. Each act of parental disobedience creates a chink in the parents' ingrained habits of submission, opening up new possibilities for the family.

The ruler's power should not be viewed as something solid and homogenous. Actually, it is nurtured by a variety of sources, some of which can be blocked or turned in a positive direction. Within the violent camp a variety of voices co-exist, some of which do not favor the perpetuation of oppression. This internal opposition, even if temporarily weak, may gain power and threaten the status quo. Gandhi and Martin Luther King, Jr., were past masters at arousing those factions within the ruling camp that supported change. To this end they repeatedly emphasized that nonviolent activists must not convey the message that the opposing side is the enemy. The enemy is *oppression*, not *the British* or *the whites*. Nonviolent resistance aims at minimizing the "us-them" polarity, so as to create a situation where more and more voices that formerly were passively identified with "them" may realign themselves and oppose the rule of force. Conversely, every step that sharpens the "us-them" polarity will increase the cohesion of the oppressors and strengthen their power.

These ideas are highly relevant for the family context. Thus we can always assume that positive tendencies, even if temporarily dormant, co-exist with negative ones within the child. Nonviolent resistance aims at awakening and enhancing these positive tendencies. To this end, one should weaken the "us-them" polarity between children and parents. For instance, it is highly desirable to stop parental accusations and constant moralizing that sharpen this polarity and cause the child to entrench himself in his negative position.

This vision of the violent or self-destructive child as many-faceted is both optimistic and realistic. It is optimistic in that positive voices, even if hard to discern, are always assumed to be present within the child. It is realistic in its assumption that the parental endeavor cannot bring about the total disappearance of the child's negative voices. Actually, there is no need to do so. It may suffice to tip the balance in favor of the positive ones.

In another therapeutic field (the treatment of suicide-prone individuals), the expression "the parliament of the mind" (Shneidman 1985) was coined to indicate that the chief aim of therapy should not be the highly unrealistic one of making the suicidal individual embrace life unconditionally. Fortunately, to prevent suicide, it is enough that the life voices attain a partial majority over the death ones. Sometimes even a minute change in this direction may suffice. Similarly, viewing the child's aggressive behavior as a result of a debate within the parliament of the child's mind leads to the formulation of a much more realistic goal than subjecting aggressiveness to "root treatment." The new goal will be to create a majority for the positive voices within the child.

INTERNAL FORCES IN NONVIOLENT RESISTANCE

Throughout history, nonviolent resistance was employed by people who had long and often passively endured the worst forms of oppression and humiliation. At first glance, it would be hard to believe that such creatures would square their shoulders and engage in a struggle. The change that makes this possible will become clear to us if we understand that the weakness of the ruled, like the strength of the ruler, is not of one cloth. Here, too, weakness is born of several factors. We described above the decisive influence of one such factor: isolation. As we saw, breaking out of isolation releases strength, sometimes in unimaginable degrees. Other processes that are also likely to favor the transition from weakness to strength are (1) unifying the powers of resistance, (2) understanding the ruler's dependence and the arbitrariness of his rule, (3) experiencing the power to resist, (4) evolving a feeling of moral and personal worth, and (5) preparing for retaliation.

1. *Unifying the powers of resistance.* To overcome fragmentation within the nonviolent side is a primary goal of nonviolent resistance. In the family arena, the very terms of nonviolent resistance offer an answer to the most common and paralyzing divisive factor between parents: the clash between the "gentle" and the "tough" approaches. Nonviolent resistance allows for cooperation even between parents who are extremely polarized in this respect, since it appeals to the legitimate feelings of both: the "gentle" parent receives a guarantee against the other's aggressive acts, while the "tough" parent receives a guarantee that surrender by the other will be averted. We clarify to the "tough" parent that the more he succeeds in curbing his own harshness, the more successfully will the "gentle" one be able to withstand her tendency to surrender. Similarly, we clarify to the "soft" parent that the more he succeeds in averting his own surrender, the more successfully will the "tough" one curb her own harshness. Under these conditions, the "tough" parent often becomes able to express gentleness and the "gentle" parent to show determination.

2. Understanding the ruler's dependence and the arbitrariness of his rule.
Nonviolent resistance is born out of the realization that all oppression is based on a tacit acquiescence by the ruled. This acquiescence is far from voluntary. On the contrary; the ruled feel it is unavoidable. Rulers invest considerable effort in engendering this feeling, and this shows how threatened they would feel by its abrogation. The establishment of oppression is a gradual process, in the course of which the ruler's misuse of the property, work, body, and life of the ruled are felt as more and more inevitable. Even the cruelest tyrannies do not achieve this goal at one blow: an ongoing "education" of the ruled is needed, to make them readier to take up their burden. A central pillar of this "education" is instilling the creed that the existing situation represents the natural state of affairs. On this line, beliefs about "white superiority," "the god-given rights of the aristocracy," or "male supremacy" have played a crucial role in the perpetuation of oppression. Nonviolent resistance challenges this "education" and stands for the awareness that oppression is intolerable and that the ruler's power is not divine but based on the sweat and the acquiescence of the ruled.

The evolution of a similar awareness plays a central role in the relationship between parents and violent or self-destructive children. Parents "learn" gradually, to take the exploitation of their work and property, the abuse of their persons, and the abrogation of their and their other children's safety for granted, stemming unavoidably as it does from the "mental disorder" or "illness" of the aggressive child. Gradually, the parents "learn" to supply this child with the means to preserve his power, territory, and freedom of action. In these processes, however, the total dependence of the child on his parents becomes manifest, for without their acquiescence and without the means they supply it is doubtful whether the exploitation could continue for even one day. The more this awareness ripens, the readier the parents grow for nonviolent resistance.

In distinction from the socio-political sphere, the rule of force in the family is perpetuated by the belief not that it reflects a natural situation, but that it is a result of pathology. Viewing the child as

"ill" leads the parents to believe she is unable to control her outbursts. The all-pervasive influence of psychology in our culture has
had a negative impact in this respect: a myriad of concepts from
the field of mental health presents the child's aggressive behavior
as an inevitable reaction to trauma and deprivation. This approach
leads to the damaging conclusion not only that parental resistance
is futile or even damaging, but also that the aggressive child should
be compensated rather than resisted. As the parents make their first
steps in nonviolent resistance, they begin realizing that the child's
misbehavior is not unavoidable. In turn, as this awareness matures,
nonviolent resistance is strengthened.

The mother of a twelve-year-old boy, who was (as she put it) "subject
to uncontrollable physical and verbal outbursts," of which she was
the target, attributed the problem to a neurological dysfunction. She
was constantly searching for medical solutions, which to that point
had not been at all effective. The parents agreed to carry out a number of sit-ins in the child's room, in which they announced to him,
that they would stay there until he suggested a way to stop the outbursts. During the sit-ins, the parents took care not to perform any
act that was liable to cause escalation. After a few sit-ins, the mother
noticed that the child was restraining himself in situations where in
the past he would have launched a violent attack. Although at that
stage the change was still limited, the mother said she now felt sure
the outbursts were not an inevitable occurrence.

3. *Experiencing the power to resist.* Gandhi claimed that the British
rule in India was perpetuated by the Indians' firmly rooted habits of
obedience. Each act of disobedience should then contribute to the
dissolution of these habits. The role of the leaders was to encourage
the followers to perform the initial steps: the courage to continue,
according to Gandhi, would be generated as a result of them. In
almost every account of nonviolent resistance, a similar process is
described: as a result of initial acts of resistance, the once pliant subjects become strengthened, and helplessness gives way to a feeling
of mission (Sharp 1973).

The automatism of obedience is a recognized factor in the relations between physically abusive husbands and their wives. Although also frequent in families with violent children, the phenomenon is far less well known.

A divorced mother of two children, ages twelve and fifteen, was both victim and witness of her elder son's violence. The mother reported that all the son's demands had to be immediately fulfilled. Any house-keeping chore would take a long time to complete, since the mother was obliged to stop her work repeatedly in order to fulfill the boy's demands. The boy, who spent most of his time lying in his room (in which the only TV set in the house was located), would call her by banging on the wall. Any delay in responding would bring immediate retaliation. The mother said, she had developed a reflex: on hearing the first knock, she would instantaneously drop whatever she was doing. The very thought of disobedience seemed unrealistic. Break-ing the automatism of obedience was defined, with her approval, as the program's first goal. The mother was not expected to find the courage for these acts of disobedience in herself: friends were invited to the house to support her initial attempts. The first expe-riences that disobedience was possible made a deep impression on her and made nonviolent resistance a real option.

We often observe that the parents' initial acts of resistance create a significant change in them, even before a change is noticeable in the child. Many parents who performed acts of nonviolent resistance, such as doing sit-ins in a child's room, standing before the door to prevent a daughter's leaving for a drug party, or arriving at the hiding place of a fugitive son reported that they felt, once again, that they existed as persons and as parents. This experience was often a turning point in the parents' view of themselves.

4. *Evolving a feeling of moral and personal worth.* One of the results of nonviolent resistance in the socio-political sphere is the transforma-tion of the subjects' sense of inferiority into a sense of self-worth and moral superiority vis-à-vis the oppressors. This feeling is preserved as long as the activists adhere strictly to nonviolence. In parent-child

relations, this sense of moral uprightness is of vital importance. Frequently, parents become paralyzed as a result of their own violent outbursts. Parental violence, even if rare, deprives the parents' demands of moral validity in their own eyes as well as in the eyes of the child or of outsiders. Nonviolent resistance allows the parents not only to be effective without being violent, but also to take corrective steps regarding their own past outbursts.

The parents of a sixteen-year-old girl, who regularly disappeared from home, stole money from them, and smoked grass on a daily basis, initiated a nonviolent resistance campaign. They wrote her a letter in which they expressed sorrow over their violent outbursts in the past. In the letter they declared that they would do all in their power to stop her destructive behavior, except for resorting to physical or verbal attacks on her. They then began a program of close parental supervision backed by a wide net of support. They quickly regained a feeling of effectiveness and worth. The girl, after some initial protests, reacted with satisfaction to the parents' "return."

5. *Preparing for retaliation.* Scenarios of potential retaliatory measures by the violent side should be developed, so as to allow for preventive steps and for rigorous planning against all forms of violent reactions by the nonviolent activists. In the socio-political sphere, these steps might include preparations for mass arrests, the development of mutual aid programs, and careful briefing of the activists against counterviolence (Sharp 1973). In addition to these practical preparations, Gandhi ascribed supreme value to spiritual preparation. This included developing the readiness to bear suffering. Gandhi held that such a readiness would not only strengthen the activists but also quicken the fall of the oppressive rule, for the violent side could not but be impressed by their opponents' readiness to endure. This would go hand in hand with a burgeoning feeling of respect for the nonviolent side. Gandhi said that once these signs of respect began to appear, the end of the oppressive rule would not be far off, for the emerging respect pointed to a new morality and to a growing readiness to forgo violence.

Parents should similarly prepare themselves and forgo the expectation that their engaging in nonviolence will bring an immediate positive response in the child. For example, performing a sit-in in the child's room is likely to "draw fire." Many children react with shouting, cursing, or physical attacks in order to drive the parents away. The parents' preparatory steps are therefore crucial for the measure's success. Thus parents should evolve a "shock absorbing" attitude against provocations and expressions of hostility. They may also invite people from outside the family to be present in the house during the sit-in; this preventative measure does much to diminish the child's violence. When the parents prepare themselves in this way, they can effectively withstand all attempts to provoke them into counterviolence. In this atmosphere, the child's verbal and physical aggressiveness gradually loses power.

Another preparatory step is to note down the telephone numbers of the children and adults with whom the child has contact. Such a list may be crucial in dealing with a child who runs away as a retaliation measure against the parents' resistance. Parents must also be prepared, on occasion, to miss a number of workdays so as to cope with a crisis.

Such preparatory steps convey to the child and to the parents themselves the message that they are willing to pay the price of their struggle. In this process the meaning of the parents' suffering is radically changed: while in the past parental suffering was just the meaningless by-product of attrition and escalation, the parents' new readiness to endure pain, tension, and attrition are a vital component in the process of change. Many parents report that this understanding endowed them with levels of endurance that would previously have seemed all but impossible. The child is also deeply affected by the parental readiness to endure: she gradually begins to doubt that she can win by violent means. Sometimes signs of respect for the parents emerge. Like in the socio-political sphere, these signs harbinger the end of violence. They attest not only to the child's external adjustment, but also to the beginning of an internal change.

A fourteen-year-old girl ran away from home and was suspected of engaging in prostitution. The parents got her to return home by getting in touch with her friends and launching a widespread search. After the girl returned home, the parents closed themselves up with her for three days. The thorough preparations by the parents, which included taking time off from work, organizing visits by friends and relatives, and making arrangements to host guests who came from another town, convinced the girl that the parents were ready to endure for long. After the three days, a compromise was reached that enabled the parents to know where she was. There were no further disappearances.

SELF-DISCIPLINE IN NONVIOLENCE

Gandhi emphasized that it is not enough to formulate principles of nonviolence; unceasing self-discipline and guidance are needed to avert the danger of violent reactions by the activists. Gandhi listed three factors that help against this danger: (1) careful preparation: the more detailed the preparation, the less the danger of being drawn into violence; (2) fighting experience: experience with nonviolent resistance tempers the activists against provocations; and (3) the availability of a nonviolent alternative, without which violent reactions might be inevitable. Gandhi argued that believers in verbal persuasion who object to any form of fight on ideological grounds actually contribute to violence, since they leave the oppressed with no alternative.

These factors are highly relevant in the family sphere:

1. *Careful preparation.* In contrast to the spontaneous reactions to which parents and children are used, nonviolent resistance is carefully planned. The parents are, for instance, instructed not to respond immediately to the child's negative acts but to "strike the iron when it is cold." Delaying the reaction is precisely what enables them to act with a minimum risk of escalation. The parents also learn to prepare in advance for the child's negative reactions to their resistance. It helps them to know that the harsher these reactions, the sooner are they exhausted.

2. *Fighting experience*. Parents taking their first steps in nonviolent resistance are in greater danger of losing control than parents who have already accumulated some experience. Therefore, especially in the initial stages, guidance and supervision are vital. It must be repeatedly emphasized that great damage will be incurred in the case of a violent outburst on their part. Apart from the potential hurt to the child, the parent who is dragged into violence is in danger of losing the support of others, of relinquishing her moral advantage, of fueling escalation, and of squelching the nonviolent voices within the child.

3. *The availability of a nonviolent alternative*. Many parents have reported that the options provided to them by nonviolent resistance helped them to overcome the feelings of frustration that in the past had made them lose control of themselves. Research upholds these reports: the more helpless the parents, the greater their danger of falling prey to violent outbursts (Bugental et al. 1989).

The following case illustrates our failure in preparing a parent for self-restraint.

The father of a sixteen-year-old girl who used to disappear from home for hours and days interpreted the need for parental presence in a highly militant way. When he returned home after the first therapeutic session, he discovered that the girl had stolen money from his wallet. The girl responded to the accusation with curses and threats. The father dragged her by force to her room in order to immediately initiate a sit-in. This led to the daughter's lodging a complaint with the police against the father, and to a countercomplaint on charges of theft by the father. The girl then persuaded her younger sister to take her side, and they both disappeared from home for two days.

THE GOALS OF NONVIOLENT RESISTANCE

Martin Luther King, Jr., attributed most of the failures of the civil rights movement in America to the fact that protests were often staged without an immediate concrete goal. Campaigns for the attainment of "freedom" or "brotherhood" are doomed to failure. The demands must always be so defined that the opponent is capable of fulfilling them. Such circumscribed goals allow for the attainment of partial victories and help sustain motivation. In addition, clear demands allow for negotiations to be conducted in parallel to non-violent resistance. Gandhi added that the immediate goals should be so defined as to symbolize the ultimate goals of the struggle.

Concerning the desired changes in the opponent, three types of goals can be defined: (1) inner conversion, (2) adjustment, and (3) nonviolent coercion (Sharp 1973). Nonviolent resistance aims at these goals simultaneously. Signs of internal conversion are manifest in the progressive awakening of objecting voices within the oppressor's camp. Signs of adjustment appear in the opponents' growing readiness for compromise. Nonviolent coercion becomes manifest when the continuation of oppression becomes literally impossible. Nonviolent resistance postulates that these three goals are mutually enhancing.

The same considerations are valid for parent-child relations. Here, too, it would be a mistake to implement nonviolent resistance for hazy goals, such as "being a good child" or "showing consideration for others." In contrast, goals such as "to stop hitting your sister" or "to return home before midnight" are clear and realistic. Parents sometimes express disappointment at these limited formulations, since they expect the child to undergo a more basic change. However, most parents know well that such a goal is unrealistic, especially so long as the child is able to rule the house with an iron fist. As in the socio-political sphere, parents can and often should strive simultaneously for conversion, adjustment, and nonviolent coercion. The goal of conversion is furthered, for instance, by the parents' nonviolent personal example, by the pressure of "public opinion," and by acts of reconciliation (see below); the goal of furthering adjustment is furthered, for instance, by sit-ins and increased parental supervision, and the goal of nonviolent coercion is achieved, for instance, when the parents withdraw the means for the child's destructive activities (e.g., taking away the car from a youngster who used it for criminal purposes).

RESPECT FOR THE OPPONENT AND
RECONCILIATION GESTURES

Leaders such as Gandhi and King did not settle for the absence of violence alone; they demanded from themselves and from their followers that the acts of resistance be accompanied, as far as humanly possible, by real respect for the adversary. This position did not characterize every nonviolent resistance movement. Some have even claimed that such demands would deter many potential followers (Sharp 1973). There is, however, a deep logic in Gandhi's and King's position: it stems from the understanding that the opponent is not made of one cloth. Acts of respect and reconciliation would then serve to strengthen the positive voices within him. Eschewing such acts or engaging in humiliating behaviors would, in contrast, strengthen the violent voices.

In the context of parent-child relations, this argument is even more valid. Our basic assumption is that the parent loves the child, even if this love is temporarily hidden from view as a result of escalation processes. Parental acts of respect and reconciliation (that do not include surrender) are thus based on existent feelings and, in turn, increase the chances that these feelings will feed positive interactions.

The parents of a twelve-year-old boy who ruled the house by means of attacks and threats initiated an extensive campaign of nonviolent resistance accompanied by gestures of respect and reconciliation. The child declared that "he would never give in to them." The parents reacted by giving the boy a certificate that stated "that it was humanly impossible to force him to surrender" and "that they were convinced that his indomitable nature would help him greatly in the future." The handing over of the certificate did not mark the end of nonviolent resistance by the parents. During a sit-in, when the boy asked the parents why they were doing it and whether they were aware that he would never give in, they answered: "Because we have no choice!" The mother initiated additional reconciliation gestures, preparing for the boy dishes that he specially liked. The boy rejected the mother's offers. The mother said it was his right to do so. After a few days, she prepared the same treats again. This time he ate them, without a word. These actions, although they did not elicit any immediate positive reaction, improved the atmosphere. The level of violence diminished and remained low afterward.

We began this chapter by describing nonviolent resistance as a fight. We concluded it by underlining the role of respect and reconciliation within the fight. This makes it clear that nonviolent resistance is the right kind of fight for relationships where love is present.

2 ESCALATION PROCESSES

An understanding of escalation processes is crucial to any confrontation with violence. Escalation processes, as we saw, are of two kinds: reciprocal and complementary (Orford 1986). In parent-child relations, these two types of escalation intensify each other, and an ongoing swing between giving in and hitting out has been shown to be a common characteristic of families with violent and self-destructive children (Bugental et al. 1989; Patterson et al. 1984). In this chapter, we attempt to trace the processes that fuel these two types of escalation and suggest possible ways of averting them.

SUBMISSION

Parents submit in order to buy quiet. This hope, however, is bound to prove illusory for, with the parents' growing submission, the child raises the price of quiet by new demands and more extreme acts (Patterson et al. 1984; Patterson, Reid, & Dishion 1992). Gradually, the parents develop a pervasive submissive attitude and come to believe that they have no way of resisting, but must adapt the life of the family – including the behavior of their other children – to the aggressive child's demands. The parents thus become the executors of the aggressive child's will, thereby harming not only themselves, but also their children.

Emerging from submission is a gradual process and it is not at all the same as "going on the war path." Actually, attempting to switch over from submission to warfare might have disastrous results, for this would heighten the level of aggression in the family and paradoxically pave the way for the parents' renewed submission. A stance of nonviolent resistance, in contrast, has a totally different impact. The parent then does not say to himself: "I'll show him!" or "I'll pay him back!" but rather "I can resist without hitting back!"

The transition from submission to nonviolent resistance gives the parents leeway to evaluate the situation ever anew and, if needed, to retreat from fruitless demands. Ironically, it is precisely those parents who are able to resist that can also make concessions. Many parents are afraid that they should guard themselves from any act that would convey weakness and that admitting an error is tantamount to accepting defeat. This attitude negates the spirit of nonviolent resistance, which demands a willingness to change direction and retreat from untoward actions. Gandhi did not hesitate to suspend a fighting campaign when this led to violence on the side of the activists. In his view, nothing was farther away from nonviolent resistance than attempts to show the other side "who's the boss."

Parents fortify themselves against submission by emerging from isolation, breaking the seal of secrecy, and developing the awareness that the child's violence is not a deterministic given. These processes, however, are hard to set in motion so long as the parents are paralyzed by fears that the child might collapse, run away, or commit suicide. Candidly confronting these fears will gradually remove the parents' grounds for submission.

The fear that the child may collapse stems from the belief that her behavior is the expression of an underlying pathology. Restraining the aggression might then bring her to a breakdown. This belief is mistaken. Violence is not the "symptom" of an illness but a means for imposing one's will. Even when violence is linked to a mental disorder (e.g., in children who suffer from attention-deficit or obsessive-compulsive disorders), it reflects the suffering child's way of ridding herself from the demands of the surroundings, gaining freedom of action, and coercing others to do her bidding. Gradually, the child comes to experience a feeling of satisfaction out of the exercise of her own power. Some may view this description of the aggressive child as pejorative. In our opinion, however, stating that children seek power does not denigrate them at all; in this they are no different from adults. People in all age groups strive to attain their goals and remove obstacles from their path. Children act so from a very tender age. With time, they learn that not all means are legitimate. This learning, however, may not occur if the child grows up without any effective external restraints. The child may then evolve the belief that any goal can be achieved if only enough force is used. In this, too, the child is similar to the adult.

The parents' fear that the child would collapse if they resisted may perhaps be allayed by telling them that in hundreds of families[1] that went over to nonviolent resistance there was not a single case of mental breakdown. Such parents who then become willing to take their first steps in nonviolent resistance will quickly discover not only that the child does not break down, but also that his outbursts can be influenced. They also find out that besides effectively restraining the child's aggressiveness, they succeed in preventing their own escalating reactions as well.

To help parents deal with their fears that the child might react by running away, one should help them act so as to minimize the threat. For instance, the parents can prepare in advance a detailed list of telephone numbers and addresses of everyone who is in contact with the child; they can enlist a network of supporters to help to search for the child in case of flight; and they can develop ways to establish communication with the child, his friends, or the friends' parents. In this manner, the child's possible running away ceases to be a paralyzing eventuality and may even be seen as an opportunity for conveying parental presence and nonviolent resistance. Besides helping them with these preparations, we also tell the parents that running away is a rare reaction to nonviolent resistance and that,

---

[1] Experience with nonviolent resistance includes: (1) 85 cases that were treated in an ongoing research project in Tel Aviv University, (2) 160 cases that were treated either by the author or by therapists who were directly supervised by him, and (3) about 150 cases that were treated by other therapists who had attended a course on nonviolent resistance by the author, and about which the author was informed.

in all our cases, it has occurred only in families where the child had already run away in the past. In addition, due to the preparations, in none of our cases did the parents remain out of touch with the child for more than a few hours.

The worst of all parental fears is the fear of suicide: the child who threatens suicide can count on paralyzing the parents and bringing them to submission. It is of course not enough to soothe the parents by telling them that child suicide is an extremely rare phenomenon. For parents living in the shadow of suicide threats, such consolations are meaningless. Instead, we must help them understand that nonviolent resistance clearly minimizes the risk of suicide. This is for a number of reasons: (1) By making their presence felt, the parents lessen the child's sense of isolation and neglect, which are central factors in suicide (Omer & Elizur 2001). Thus parents who live in fear of entering the child's room or what the child defines as her private sphere should be reminded that their re-entrance signifies not only parental invasiveness, but also parental availability and protection. In effect, many children react positively to the parents' renewed presence, even if initially they put up a fight against it. (2) Nonviolent resistance helps parents to prevent the escalation that might lead to suicidal threats and attempts; and (3) as the parents emerge from isolation, they evolve a supportive net that serves as a protective barrier against the child's suicidal tendencies.

A violent adolescent girl, who routinely threatened suicide as a way to put pressure on her parents, received a number of phone calls from relatives and friends of the parents declaring their support for the parents' efforts to stop the violence and the threats. After the third call, she came out of her room with a grin and playfully threatened: "I'll kill you, Daddy!" The father felt that the grin and the playful tone said much more than the words.

"WHO'S THE BOSS?"

Dominance orientation is the tendency of people to view relationships in terms of "who's the boss?" The more pronounced this tendency, the greater the danger of escalation. Thus parents who are high in dominance orientation were found to be particularly liable to violent outbursts (Bugental et al. 1989, 1993, 1997). This holds true for the dominance-oriented child as well. If one of the sides in the relationship (in our case, the parent) succeeds in curbing her own dominance orientation, the danger of escalation lessens considerably. Our goal in working with parents is then to help them curb their dominance orientation without giving in to the child's strong-arm methods. Nonviolent resistance provides the answer, since it allows a determined parental stand without overtones of "bossiness."

The child's dominance orientation manifests itself from an early age. Small children often use expressions such as: "I'm the king!" or "I'm the strongest!" As they grow up, the style changes to expressions like: "You just try and stop me!" or "You think you can tell me what to do?" Parents, too, have their characteristic ways to express this tendency. For instance: "You'll do what I say, or else!" or "You think you're the boss here? Wait and see!" This parental attitude often emerges in the early stages of acquaintance with nonviolent resistance. For example, some parents react to our suggestion of reconciliation gestures by saying: "But then she'll think she has won!" or "He'll see this as a sign of weakness!" Also in defeat parents sometimes express their tendency to think in terms of "who's the boss?" They may then say: "We can't stop her: she's stronger than us!" It is as if there were only two possibilities: either the parents win or the child wins. This attitude must lead to attempts at mutual subjugation, that is, to escalation.

These considerations help us to understand why programs of reward and punishment are often ineffectual with adolescents, especially with those with a strong dominance orientation. Research on parent training programs centered on reward and punishment shows that as the child grows older, parents drop out of the program in increasing numbers (Dishion & Patterson 1992; Patterson, Dishion, & Chamberlain 1993). This higher drop-out rate is probably due to the older child's stronger resistance to these programs. In effect, for a dominance-oriented child, the parent's success in directing her behavior by means of reward and punishment shows that the parent is the boss. The punishment is then more than just a punishment, for the child who changes her behavior in its wake feels not only punished but defeated. Viewed in this way, even a reward can become a negative experience for a dominance-oriented child. Such a child may then try to pocket the reward without paying its price (i.e., acknowledging that the parent makes the rules), by showing that the reward does not obligate her to anything. The best way to prove this is to behave as badly as possible immediately after receiving the reward. Thus a boomerang effect is created. Such reactions are particularly likely when the parent giving the child the reward makes statements such as "We are now turning over a new leaf!" The child may then feel obligated to disappoint the parent's expectations. We would predict that the larger the reward and the more festive the declaration of a "new leaf," the worse the subsequent behavior of the dominance-oriented child.

After a stormy fight with his mother, a fifteen-year old boy stole money from his mother's wallet and ran away from home. The mother found him and convinced him to return home, promising he would not be punished. The boy controlled his aggressive behavior for a few days, whereupon the mother decided to reinforce him by announcing a ski vacation. She added that this would turn over a new leaf in their relationship. In the days before the trip, the boy showed that he had no intention of fulfilling the mother's expectations. The mother was caught in a dilemma regarding the vacation, but in the end decided to go despite her disappointment at her son's behavior. The boy behaved very aggressively to her throughout the vacation and even more so when they returned home.

The steps of nonviolent resistance are carefully devised so as to avoid any overweening show of authority or demand for surrender. Their message is not "You will do as I wish, or else," but rather "I'm not prepared to continue like this! My duty is to do all in my power to resist, except for attacking you!" This message is not lacking in power and implies a tacit threat. The threat, however, differs on many counts from that of the parent who wants to show he is the boss: (1) the parent declares in advance that he will not use violence; (2) the message focuses not on the child ("You will change your behavior!") but on the parent ("I am no longer prepared..."); (3) the tacit threat does not involve a sovereign punishment imposed "from above" but expresses the parent's moral duty to resist destructive behaviors; and (4) the emphasis is not on the result ("You will behave differently!") but on the action itself ("It is my duty to resist!"). In this way, the parental acts are cleaned of their dominant overtones.

Gandhi expressed this spirit of determination without dominance in a letter to Lord Irwin, the British Viceroy, in which he communicated his decision to resist the British salt monopoly. After declaring that India had the duty to do all in her power to free herself from the "embrace of death" of the British Empire, Gandhi announced that he and his followers had no alternative but to initiate a wide-ranging campaign of nonviolent resistance against the monopoly. He ended the letter paradoxically: "This letter is not in any way intended as a threat but as a simple and sacred duty peremptory on a civil resister" (Sharp 1960: 200–204). The paradox consists in the concurrent announcement of a fighting campaign and the declaration that this was no threat. The paradox may, however, be resolved, if we consider that Gandhi's threat is very different from an ordinary threat: (1) threats do not usually include an explicit declaration of nonviolence; (2) Gandhi says not, "You will do this, or else," but "We have no choice, but..."; and (3) there is no hint of willfulness in Gandhi's words ("This is what I want!") but an expression of duty ("The simple, holy duty..."). The message conveyed by a routine dominant threat is "I will punish you if you don't do as I wish!" Gandhi's nondominant threat states: "You are stronger than I am, but my supreme duty is to resist you in a nonviolent way!" The difference is profound enough for us to define Gandhi's threat as "a threat in a nonthreatening spirit." Such a threat is free of the need to show "who's the boss."

In working with parents in this spirit, we try to help them to stop all dominant threats and renounce all attempts to show the child "who's the boss." Parents learn gradually to avoid thinking in terms of "who's the boss?" Thus, when they are still green in the ways of nonviolent resistance, they may remain focused on the child's reactions and keep asking, "Who won?" Typical parental reactions at this stage are "We tried that and it didn't help! She didn't give a damn about us!" or "How wonderfully he reacted! He was really a sweetie after the sit-in!" Gradually, the parents learn to focus more on their own acts and less on the child's reactions. They may then say things like: "I managed to sit quietly in her room for 40 minutes!" or "I didn't yell back when she yelled at me!" The most advanced stage is reached when the parents engage in nonviolent resistance not only to cause the child to improve her behavior, but because it feels right to them: they then act so because it makes them feel less exploited, helpless, or impulsive and more at one with themselves. Parents who reach this stage bring about a great improvement in the home atmosphere. The child then changes her behavior not as a direct response to sanctions or demands but so as to fit into the new atmosphere.

The father of a fifteen-year-old boy had the following conversation with his son in the course of a sit-in.

Son: You'll never be able to tell me what to do, even if you bring all your friends, all the people in your office and the whole world!

Father: I know I can't tell you what to do.

Son: Are you trying to make a fool of me? Then why are you doing this?

Father: Because I have to.

Son: Okay, you'll see! You'll be sorry! You won't see me again! You'll suffer a hundred times worse!

Father: We'll suffer, but not alone.

This father radiated determination and responsibility without trying to subjugate his son. The "who's the boss?" attitude vanished altogether and with it the threat of escalation.

Together with a "who's the boss?" attitude goes the tendency to engage in "games of pride." Games of pride are interactions based on the assumption that if the other does not show respect, one loses pride. This assumption leads the offended side to try and force the other to change her behavior or, alternatively, to hurt her sufficiently so as to balance the score. As in any competitive game, both sides continually attend to the score and try to outmaneuver each other.

A common game of pride involves the parents' "obligatory" reactions to the child's insulting behavior. In this game, so long as the child does not stop calling the parents names or making offensive gestures, the parents' pride balance will remain negative. They then feel obligated to punish the child until he stops the behavior and asks for forgiveness. The punishment has a double goal: to stop the insults and to even the score. If the insults continue or are resumed after a break, the parents must punish harder. This parental game of pride brings the child to evolve a counterstrategy. For example, he may lay low for a while, until the parents are less alert or bothered by other things. At this propitious time, the child may return to his insulting behavior. The parents now feel doubly offended (as both their pride and their trust were injured) and feel that they must react particularly harshly. In this way, parents who say: "You will stop calling me names, or else" almost inevitably initiate an escalation process.

But what should the parents do? Relinquish their pride? This question is itself phrased in terms of games of pride. Nonviolent resistance suggests an alternative. By engaging in nonviolent resistance, the parents convey to the child that they will neither be passive targets for insults nor be provoked into hostile escalation. Here the emphasis is no longer on the results (stopping the insults); the parents, instead, find *in their own acts* the source of their self-respect. Thus once they initiate nonviolent resistance, they feel much less insulted by the child's name calling, since their self-respect now stems from their own behavior. The parents may even tell the child that they have power not to stop the insults, but only to restore their self-esteem by nonviolent resistance. A similar process happens with nonviolent

activists in the socio-political arena: once Gandhi and his followers initiated nonviolent resistance, the British policemen's insults or
blows could no longer wound their self-esteem. From that moment,
the activists' feeling of worth stemmed from their own actions and
not from the way the British behaved toward them.

This attitude creates a new situation. The insults, whose goal is to
provoke anger and hurt, lose much of their effect. The child may
of course occasionally check out whether the "magic" of the insults
has returned. The parents must then remind themselves that their
self-esteem is a function of their own behavior and not of the child's
insulting or not insulting them.

EMOTIONAL AROUSAL

The higher the emotional arousal of the two sides in a conflict situation, the higher the risk of escalation. If, however, the arousal of
even only one of the sides is lowered, the risk of escalation is much reduced. This has been repeatedly demonstrated. (1) When two animals
are in conflict, chemically reducing the arousal of one of them greatly
reduces the other's aggressiveness (Cairns, Santoyo, & Holly 1994).
(2) Spouses who become mutually aroused in the course of routine
arguments are in high risk of divorce; conversely, if one of the sides
succeeds in dampening his arousal, the risk diminishes significantly
(Gottman, 1998; Levenson & Gottman 1983, 1985). (3) Parents who
are easily aroused provoke violent reactions in their children and react themselves violently in conflict situations (Bugental et al. 1993).
These findings justify the popular saying: "It takes two to tango."

High emotional arousal leads parents and children to evolve both
reciprocal and complementary escalation. This is so because parents
often become alarmed by the intensity of their (and the child's) negative feelings, while the aggressive child is far less afraid of his own
outbursts. As a result of this imbalance, the parents often prefer to
submit. Reciprocal escalation thus heightens the risk of the parents'
giving in in the next round of the conflict. Giving in, in turn, increases the parents' frustration and anger, thus bringing them back
to reciprocal escalation.

The role of emotional arousal in escalation underlies the precept: "Strike the iron when it is cold!" At the time the negative behaviors appear, both sides are in a heightened emotional state and, therefore, are highly liable to escalation. Thus, we enjoin parents to delay the measures of nonviolent resistance for a few hours or a day after the negative event. Of course, the parents must try and stop the child's damaging activities immediately (e.g., stop him from hitting a sibling). What is delayed to a later stage is the educational and disciplinary measures. This precept contrasts with the behavioral rule, according to which the parents should reward or punish the child's actions immediately. Our experience has shown that, besides holding less risk of escalation, delayed parental reactions are no less effective than immediate ones.

The mother of a ten-year-old boy asked what she should do when the child cursed her and kicked her. The therapist suggested performing a sit-in later in the day, thus acting according to the principle: "Strike the iron when it is cold!" The mother asked what she should do during the attack. Should she defend herself physically? Should she call for help immediately? The therapist asked whether she could defend herself without hitting back, and the mother said she doubted it. The therapist asked if there was an immediate way of getting help, and the mother answered there wasn't. The only thing the mother felt capable of doing was breaking off contact with the child by going outside or closing herself in her room for a few minutes. However, she feared that by so acting, she would be conveying weakness. The therapist clarified that there was no need for her to be stronger than the child. Breaking off contact for a few minutes and planning with suitable help a sit-in later in the day would be resistance enough.

WORDINESS

The way parents express themselves verbally is liable to contribute to both reciprocal and complementary escalation. Parental entreaties and apologies, for instance, are common submissive behaviors that may lead to complementary escalation. Furthermore, when the child reacts dismissively to the entreaties and apologies, the parents may be provoked to react in kind; we then have reciprocal escalation. Parental accusations, threats, and screams are hostile behaviors that fuel reciprocal escalation. This, in turn, may scare the parents back into submission. In this way, submissive parental speech leads to hostile speech, and vice versa.

A common type of ineffectual parental speech is the so-called reasonable argument, in which the parents try to demonstrate to the child that she is wrong or that she is lying. For example, parents often try to back up their claims by collecting evidence that the child stole, lied, or smoked grass. With the dominance-oriented child, these claims may lead to escalation, for she often reacts to the presented evidence with blunt denial and increased hostility.

The father of a thirteen-year-old girl suspected her of stealing money from the cash register of the family shop. He systematically tracked the money and, on noticing the disappearance of a large sum, invited the girl for a talk and confronted her with his calculations. The girl denied the charges. The father noticed her overstuffed wallet on the table and asked her to show him its contents. The girl pocketed the wallet and said that the father had no right to invade her privacy. The father threatened she would not be allowed to leave the house unless she showed him the wallet. The girl showered him with curses, and threw a vase at him. The father tried to hold her by force, and she bit him.

A particularly problematic type of parental speech in cases of aggressive adolescents is moralizing. Adolescents are averse to moralizing because they see it as an attempt to change their identity. Building an independent identity is a central developmental goal of adolescence. The parents' attempt to change the adolescent's evolving value system is therefore often experienced as particularly invasive. For this reason, many adolescents react better to a clear-cut declaration of parental limits than to the parents' attempt to make them accept the limits as good for them. This creates a paradoxical situation: strictly forbidding the child to do something dangerous is experienced as less invasive than reasonably explaining why it is dangerous.

Only when the parent-child relationship is relatively harmonious can the two conduct fruitful debates on loaded topics. When the relationship is troubled by conflict, almost any such discussion will lead to escalation. We thus advise parents to keep discussion of controversial topics to a minimum. Silence is a valuable asset in nonviolent resistance, but in no way should this be the silence of detachment. Parents usually feel they have only two alternatives to the child's provocation: reacting sharply or ignoring it entirely. Nonviolent resistance offers a third one: the silence of parental presence. When faced with the child's provocation, the parents take action in silence and thus manifest their resistance, while staying in contact.

POLARIZATION AND MUTUAL DETACHMENT

Polarization is a process in which both sides increasingly view each other as mutually antithetic. "Him-me" or "us-them" comes to express an ineradicable opposition. The more acute the polarization, the deeper the sides' entrenchment in uncompromising positions. This process is generally accompanied by a mutual cutting off. Parents break off contact for various reasons: a desire to punish ("Get out of my sight!"), a feeling of offense ("I won't talk to him again until he says he's sorry!"), or a sense of despair.

Children and especially adolescents often respond in kind when the parents polarize the situation or break off contact. Thus, every parental address that begins with an accusing "You!" strengthens the child's hostility and self-entrenchment. In their readiness to break off contact, adolescents are especially liable to go to extremes. Thus, parents who break off contact for a day may unwittingly incite the child to do the same for much longer periods. Cut-offs tend so much to escalate that it is not unusual for adolescents and their parents to remain disconnected for years.

Being the underside of parental presence, nonviolent resistance counters all kinds of cut-off. In this respect, the nonviolent struggle of parents differs from that of political activists: where parents want to become close and present to their children, Gandhi surely did not strive to become closer to the British! This difference lends a special hue to parental resistance: it becomes operative in the very act of establishing parental presence, that is, parents resist the child's destructiveness simply by being there. Presence also makes for the difference between nonviolent resistance and routine punishments. Thus, whereas in routine punishments the parent stands "over and outside" when administering the sanction, in the act of nonviolent resistance, the parent stands "by and with" the child (even when the manifestation of resistance is highly unpleasant). Similarly, while in the more usual varieties of disciplinary action the parent sets the child a limit, in nonviolent resistance the parent is himself the limit.

One of the means to reduce polarization between parents and children is to involve mediators. The emergence from isolation and secrecy allows parents to find potential mediators, where previously candidates to the role were hard to find. Mediators can reduce polarization, for instance, by evolving with the child honorable solutions, conveying positive messages from the parents, or effecting compromises. These roles are especially important in times of crisis. A central precept of nonviolent resistance is that, in a crisis, mediators should be immediately brought in, so as to defuse the danger of escalation.

An eighteen-year-old boy left home as a result of a stormy argument with his mother. He announced from his hiding place that he would not return home or talk to his parents ever again. The parents made a telephone round, contacting a large number of the boy's friends. Among these was also the boy in whose home the runaway was staying. The parents asked to meet this friend and his mother, who were both surprised to find out that they were not at all the monsters the boy had described. As a result of this contact, the friend and his mother decided to help patch up the severed relations between the boy and his parents. With the help of two other of the boy's friends, who also thought he had overreacted, the runaway agreed to return home. The inclusion of his peers in the net of helpers not only lessened polarization, but also allowed the boy to return home without loss of face.

NARROWNESS AND RIGIDITY

With growing hostility, the mutual relations between parent and child become increasingly rigid and narrow. The positive aspects of the relationship gradually disappear. The conflict is all that remains.

In a process of escalation each side tries to force the other to conform to his wishes but in the very attempt restricts his own freedom of action (Cairns et al. 1994). The further this process advances, the harder it is to change one's behavior or withdraw from the interaction. At the beginning there is still a feeling of self-direction, but as the grip tightens, a growing sense of being coerced evolves. In this situation both parent and child come to view their actions as unavoidable. Therapists can help parents challenge this belief, loosen their sense of entrapment, and restore their initiative.

Nonviolent resistance rescues the parents from their narrowness and rigidity by (1) releasing them from the obligation to react immediately, (2) countering the self-restrictive thinking in terms of "an eye for an eye" (Gandhi commented that "an eye for an eye" can make the whole world blind), (3) neutralizing games of pride, and (4) offering a positive alternative, where formerly there seemed to be only two negative ones. Furthermore, reconciliation gestures allow for the replacement of the vicious circles of hostility by positive circles of affection. As a result, many parents (and children) have reported a renewed sense of freedom. A mother said: "I stopped reacting like a robot and got back my sense of initiative!" A fifteen-year-old boy said, "I can't believe this is really my father! I didn't know he was capable of such behavior!"

RECONCILIATION GESTURES

A recent sensational discovery in ethological research involves the vital function of reconciliation gestures in preventing escalation among monkeys and apes (de Waal 1993). In the wake of a violent conflict between two individuals, there is a high probability that the attacker, the victim, or both will try to reestablish closeness by means of reconciliation gestures, such as hugging, kissing on the mouth, or offering an open hand. These actions greatly reduce the risk that the hostilities will be resumed. Sometimes a third party initiates the reconciliation. For example, the female partner of one of the rivals may approach each of them and pull them together. When both males are standing side by side, the female leaves quietly. In this situation, one of the males almost invariably initiates reconciliation moves. Alternatively, the female mate of the attacking male might perform reconciliatory gestures toward the victimized male, as if in the name of the attacker. According to de Waal, the objective of these gestures is to help preserve valuable relationships. It was found that the closer the relationship between the individuals before the conflict, the higher the chances that reconciliation gestures will occur.

Reconciliation gestures may play a similar function in parent-child conflicts. Thus small children spontaneously perform such gestures toward their parents after an angry outburst by them or by the parents (Potegal & Davidson 1997). Experience shows that such spontaneous gestures are less frequent with aggressive adolescents. However, precisely in these cases, reconciliation moves initiated by the parents (in parallel to nonviolent resistance) can help to minimize hostility and to broaden the basis of the relationship. In our program, parents have often reported that initiating reconciliation moves, far from weakening their determination, actually strengthened their adherence to nonviolent resistance. This reaction is understandable: the reconciliation gestures released the parents from the role of "the bad guys."

Parental reconciliation gestures can also be undertaken through the mediation of a third party. Thus, a family friend can pass a message to an adolescent who refuses to receive any communication from her parents. Mediators can also perform reconciliation gestures, stating that they are being done with the parents' consent and support. The child's friends can be excellent candidates for this role. Thus, a friend who tries to convince an aggressive child that it is not dishonorable to accept the parents' reconciliation gestures is likely to be more effective than any adult.

One of the objections parents raise to reconciliation gestures is that they may convey weakness. This feeling reflects the parents' tendency to think in terms of "who's the boss?" On these lines, anything that does not convey toughness conveys weakness. However, as they gain experience in nonviolent resistance, the parents learn to differentiate between reconciliation and submission. The gains for both sides are clear, for a parent who can make a reconciliation move a few hours after a determined show of nonviolent resistance demonstrates to herself and to the child that she has freed herself from the "an eye for an eye" and the "who's the boss?" mindsets.

ESCALATION: AN INTEGRATIVE MODEL

Escalation makes the behavior of the sides more and more extreme and lessens their degrees of freedom. The person who is caught in such a process experiences a worsening of relations and a restriction of options. In the figure below, this restriction and worsening are depicted by the gradual narrowing of the upper cone. The appearance of new options and the improvement that results from de-escalation are depicted by the widening of the lower cone.

Along the time axis, we distinguish between escalation that takes place within the same conflict event ("episodic escalation") and escalation that takes place in the course of a succession of events ("ongoing escalation"). The more dangerous kind of escalation is the ongoing one, since it is responsible for the relationship's progressive deterioration. Thus although nonviolent resistance aims at minimizing both kinds of escalation, one must never try to reduce episodic escalation at the cost of ongoing escalation. In other words, quiet in the short run should never be bought at the price of a worsening in the long run.

From the parents' point of view, every event can end up in one of three ways: submission, collision, or nonviolent resistance. When an event ends in parental submission, we may witness a lull in episodic escalation (since submission "buys" a temporary quiet), but at the price of ongoing escalation. When an event ends in mutual collision,

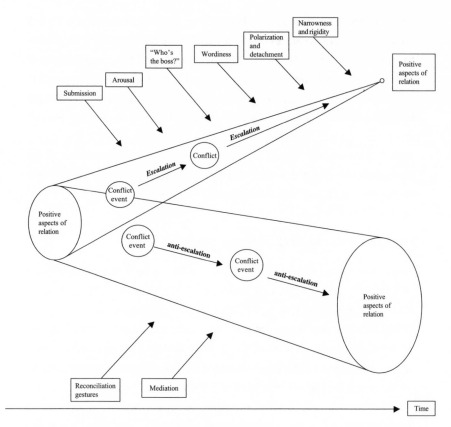

The Escalation Model

we witness both episodic and ongoing escalation. When the parents succeed in avoiding both submission and collision by an effective show of nonviolent resistance, we may witness episodic escalation (because the child may try to force submission or provoke a collision), but the ongoing escalation will be countered.

The major factors that contribute to collision or submission are a "who's the boss?" attitude, games of pride, high emotional arousal, negative parental speech (self-justification, preaching, accusations, threats, insults, and shouting), mutual polarization, mutual cut-offs, and relational narrowing. These factors appear in the diagram as arrows above the upper cone. Factors that reduce the risk of collision are the introduction of mediators and the performance of reconciliation gestures. These factors appear in the diagram as arrows under the lower cone. The model predicts that parental adherence to a policy of nonviolent resistance that is enriched by the inclusion of mediators and the performance of reconciliation gestures is the surest way to widen the relationship and counter escalation processes.

3 THE PARENTS' INSTRUCTION MANUAL

Co-authored by Uri Weinblatt and Carmelit Avraham-Krehwinkel

Aggressive and self-destructive children exhibit a long list of behaviors that severely challenge parents and educators: provocations, angry outbursts, risky and self-destructive acts, violence against others, self, and property, school drop-out, truancy, sexual promiscuousness, drug abuse, lies, thefts, and blackmail are some of the behaviors that baffle and shake even the most patient and loving caretakers. Parents commonly feel that their attempts to change the child's behavior, even those that are warmly recommended by professionals, misfire and seem actually to make matters worse. In their confusion, parents may waver between giving in and fighting back, both of which lead to further escalation. Under these conditions, the home, which should be a safe haven for the whole family, comes to resemble a battlefield. Even the smallest disagreement risks flaring up into a major eruption.

Understanding the process of escalation turns out to be one of the keys for coping with such situations. We distinguish between two varieties of escalation: (1) "reciprocal escalation," in which the child's and the parents' angry acts feed each other in a vicious cycle, and (2) "complementary escalation," in which the child's threats lead to parental giving in, which in turn increases the child's demands and threats, and so forth. To make things worse, the two kinds of escalation are mutually enhancing, so that the more the parents give in, the more frustrated and angry they get, thus coming closer and closer to an uncontrollable outburst. On the other hand, the stronger the mutual hostile outbursts, the more frightened the parents become, so that they gradually get closer to the point where they are willing to give in. In such atmosphere, no wonder the parents become less and less capable of expressing or even feeling their love for their child. Nonviolent resistance is a way of getting out of this bind.

NONVIOLENT RESISTANCE

Nonviolent resistance aims at enabling you to stop the child's destructive behaviors without engendering escalation. We define nonviolent resistance as a series of activities that convey the message of "I am no longer prepared to continue with this situation, and will do all in my power so as to change it – except by attacking you physically or verbally."

Nonviolent resistance is characterized by the following principles:

1. A firm stance on issues of violence, risk-taking, and antisocial behaviors.

2. Absolute avoidance of all physical or verbal attacks.

Nonviolent resistance is what gives you a moral and practical basis to make yourself present in the child's life and to supervise his doings. Nonviolent resistance prevents and reduces escalation.

The purpose of nonviolent resistance is to restore your presence as a parent in the child's life. We believe that a clear and firm parental presence is the chief means for developing a good relationship with your children. The parental authority we aim for is based not on the parents' being physically stronger than the child but on their being determinedly present in her life. The more you establish your presence, the greater the chances your child will give up her destructive patterns and a dialogue will once again be established between you and your child.

WITHSTANDING PROVOCATIONS AND THE PRINCIPLE OF DELAYED REACTION

To prevent escalation and put a stop to useless power struggles, you must avoid needless confrontations. But children who have learned that they can have their way by threats and violence will try to draw you into confrontations. Power-oriented children know that they can gain from a confrontation also when they don't "win," for getting you to lose control may serve them as a justification for continuing with their aggressive behavior. Children's aggressive behavior is often due to escalation habits – that is, they have learned that when they don't get what they want, they may get it by behaving more extremely.

We may assume that you also have developed escalation habits. You also have a "short fuse" that does not allow you to remain calm in a situation of conflict and causes you to lose control. Even talking too much may lead to escalation. In effect, parents, who are easily provoked to power clashes with their children, tend to do a lot of talking, such as arguing, moralizing, and threatening. Most of this parental talk leads to escalation.

Children often ignore the parents' attempts to explain, moralize, and argue with them. Sometimes they react to the parental attempts with open contempt and sarcasm. In such situations, the more you talk, the more helpless you will feel. For this reason, remember: Too much talking comes from helplessness and leads to escalation. A short and clear prohibition is better than lengthy explanations, arguments, and sermons. Remember also that threats ("If ..., then!") lead to counterthreats. Therefore, learn to withstand provocations, avoid confrontations, and abstain from arguing, moralizing, threatening, and screaming.

One useful way to avoid unnecessary confrontations and prevent escalation is to follow the principle of delayed reaction: the thought that you must immediately respond to every demand, complaint, accusation, or provocation by the child is mistaken. It may be much better to practice delaying your reaction. Therefore, give yourself time to plan your response. When in doubt, it is best to keep quiet and not react. Silence gains you time and allows the aggressive child "to waste ammunition."

Silence is not submission. If you wish, you can preface your silence with a few words, such as: "I don't like this and I'm going to think about it." This statement must be made without any hint of a threat, but as the establishment of a fact. After you do this a few times, the child will understand that your silence is not the end of the matter. Silence without submission is more effective than any sermon or argument. Your silence will make it clear that you are no longer cooperating with the child's invitations to conflict. Constructive silence involves no cutting off on your part. You stay silent, but you stay present as a parent.

When you find that your patience is being badly taxed, repeat to yourself quietly: "Don't be provoked, don't be provoked, don't be provoked!"

These practices will help you evolve the capacity to endure and withstand attacks. With this attitude you can allow the child's attacks to waste themselves. As we see below, this capacity is further abetted by practical steps to protect yourselves, the family, and the child himself against his extreme behaviors. Developing this attitude will help you deal with two emotional states that often bring you to give in or to hit back, namely, despair and anger. Despair makes you try to buy peace and quiet at any price; anger makes you respond to the child in kind. In contrast, the nonviolent readiness to endure and withstand attacks will allow you to persist with nonviolent resistance and avoid giving in or hitting back.

THE ANNOUNCEMENT

Once you opt for nonviolent resistance, it is important to convey your intentions to your child in the clearest possible way. You should tell the child that you cannot put up any more with his present behavior and that you no longer will remain alone but will inform the people around you about the situation and ask for their help. This policy of "cards on the table" will give you a moral and a practical advantage. Thus, if the child blames you for "betraying" him to others, you will know that you made yourself clear beforehand. This will help you feel justified, in spite of the accusations.

The announcement symbolizes a turning point for the whole family. From this point on, you are committed to yourself, to your spouse, to your helpers, and to your children.

Form and Timing of the Announcement

The announcement should be made at a relatively quiet time and be delivered in a clear and nonthreatening tone. It is preferable that the parent who until then displayed the more lenient attitude toward the child be the one that makes the announcement. This conveys the message that the parents are at one on the matter and that something has already begun to change. It is also a good idea to read the announcement from a written page. Thus if the child refuses to listen, the page with the announcement can be delivered by hand. Reading from a written page lends a formal validity to the announcement that is not at all detrimental to the desired effect.

If you fear the child may react violently, invite a third person (friend or relative) to be present. This will much reduce the risk of violence.

If at the time there is no communication between you and the child, bring in a third person as a mediator. This person will then make the announcement to the child in your name.

The Child's Reaction to the Announcement

It is quite probable that the child will react to the announcement with indifference, contempt, or aggression. You should react with firm silence to any of these responses. Responding to provocations with a determined silence will characterize many of your dealings with the child from now on.

The Content of the Announcement

Decide on a small number of unacceptable behaviors that you want to include in the announcement. Use a matter-of-fact rather than a judgmental language. For example, don't say, "We cannot put up with your cruel abuse!" Say rather: "We cannot put up with your hitting of your sister and your mother!"

A Suggested Format

"Violence has made life unbearable for us. We cannot and do not want to live like this any longer. We will do all we can to change the situation – except attacking you physically or verbally. To this end, we decided on the following:

We shall be consistently present in your life.

We shall no longer remain alone with the problem but shall appeal to relatives and friends, tell them openly what is going on, and ask for their help and support.

We shall determinedly oppose the following behaviors: ———.

We have no intention whatsoever of subduing you or gaining control over you. This message is not a threat, but an expression of our supreme duty as parents and human beings."

THE SIT-IN

One of the simplest and clearest manifestations of nonviolent resistance is the sit-in. This activity allows you to manifest parental presence without escalating or losing control. Its purpose is to convey to the child that you won't put up with her destructive acts anymore.

Enter the child's room at a convenient time for you, when the child is in the room. Don't do this immediately in the wake of a display of aggressive behavior by the child, but a few hours or even a day later. This delay helps to prevent escalation ("Strike the iron when it is cold!"). Shut the door after you, and sit down in a way that prevents the child's leaving the room (e.g., the father sits in front of the door). After sitting down, say to the child: "We are not prepared to put up with this behavior anymore (describe specifically the unacceptable behavior). We are here to find a way to solve the problem. We will sit and wait until you suggest a solution." You should then remain quiet and wait for suggestions. If any are forthcoming, consider them positively. If the child answers you with accusations ("It's my brother's fault!"), demands ("If you buy me a TV set, I'll stop!"),

The Parents' Instruction Manual

or threats ("Then I'll run away from home!"), do not be provoked into an argument but continue sitting quietly. You may remark that what the child has said is not a solution, but by all means avoid being drawn into any discussion. All discussions carry a high risk of escalation.

Avoid blaming, sermonizing, threatening, or screaming. Wait patiently and do not be provoked into a verbal or physical struggle. Time, silence, and the fact that you remain in the room convey the message of parental presence.

If the child makes any positive suggestion (even a very small one), ask him a few clarifying questions in a positive spirit and then leave the room, saying that the suggestion will be given a chance. Do not question the child's proposal suspiciously. Do not threaten that you will return to sit in the room if the suggestion fails to materialize. If the child has already made the same suggestion in a previous sit-in, you may answer: "You've already made that suggestion and it didn't help. Now we need a suggestion that will work better!" If the child does not make a suggestion, stay in the room for one hour, then leave without any threat or warning that you will be back. When you leave, you can say: "We still haven't found a solution."

Points to remember:

1. You must plan ahead the best time to sit in the room (you must have one hour free).

2. You must specifically indicate what you want, for example, "We are no longer willing to put up with your hitting your sister, calling her names, and ridiculing her." Very general or hazy goals are not helpful.

3. If you anticipate that the child may respond with physical violence, it is advisable to have one or two other persons in the house (friends or relatives), but not in the room. In such a case, the child should be told: "Since we were afraid that you would be violent, we invited X to serve as a witness."

4. If the child behaves violently despite the presence of the witnesses outside the room, you should ask them to enter the room. Experience with dozens of cases showed that the presence of a third party almost invariably stopped the violence.

5. After the sit-in is over, the daily routine is to be continued without mentioning the sit-in or the desired change.

Your child will not be happy about your entering her room. The following are a few common reactions of children and ways for dealing with them in the spirit of nonviolent resistance:

Trying to drive you out. The child may try to drive you out of the room, for example, by screaming at you. The best thing to do is to stay silent. Remaining silent is no sign of weakness. On the contrary, the initiative is now in your hands and staying silent means that you refuse to be drawn into the child's provocations. In case the child tries to drive you out by physical means, protect yourselves without hitting back. Remember to invite a third person to be present during the sit-in if you have any fear that the child will become violent. If there is no third party present and you cannot protect yourself without hitting back, then it is advisable to stop the sit-in, knowing that you can resume it later in the presence of witnesses. It is important that you develop the readiness to stop any activity that leads to violence. This is not a sign of submission, but a tactical retreat that allows you to come back when you are better prepared.

Setting conditions. The child may set conditions to the desired improvement, such as, "I'll do what you want if you buy me such and such." Answer that you cannot accept the suggestion. Do not give any grounds for your refusal, as this would lead you into an argument. After this short answer, resume your silent sitting.

Ignoring you. By this response, the child tries to show you that the activity is having no effect on him. He might, for instance, turn on the television or play with the computer. In this case, turn off the equipment once. If he turns it on again, do not turn it off (for this would lead to a recursive escalation), but wait in the room until the end of the hour. The next time, before entering the child's room, turn off the electrical appliances or remove the mouse from the computer for the duration of the sit-in. The child may also lie down and pretend to sleep. If this happens, just continue the sit-in. Time passes very slowly when the child pretends to be asleep! Even if he really does fall asleep, the sit-in should be continued. The child's falling asleep with you in the room may well be a first sign that the relationship is changing.

Screaming to get external attention. The aim of this behavior is to embarrass you before the neighbors. If you feel anxious about this possibility, warn the neighbors in advance and explain your intentions to them. It helps to give the neighbors a copy of these instructions.

Attempting to involve you in an argument. In this way, the child attempts to bring you back to your usual talkative role. One way of doing this is to claim not to understand what you want. Any attempts to explain beyond a very short statement will diminish the effectiveness of the sit-in.

Making a suggestion. Any positive suggestion by the child, even the mere promise to try her best, should be accepted. Once the suggestion is made, leave the room without setting conditions or issuing a warning. You need not worry about the child's having "tricked" you into leaving the room, for, if the problem remains, you can always return to the room and do another sit-in. The next time, of course, a new and better suggestion must be made for the sit-in to be stopped. You should keep in mind that children often change their behavior without having made any suggestion, for many children would see such a suggestion as a token of submission. They would then prefer to change their behavior without giving you such a token. Remember, the goal of the sit-in is not to win, but to manifest parental presence. The working factor is your being there and not the child's suggestion.

The sit-in begins a change process in the child and in you. The child will begin adapting to the new situation. As for you, being able to enter the child's room and to stay there without being drawn into an argument or an escalating bout will begin changing your sense of your abilities. Many parents say that the sit-in gave them back the feeling that they exist. Through the sit-in, your place in the family map begins to change.

One more point to remember: the goal of the sit-in is not to make the child act nicely during the procedure. Thus, even if the child behaves obstreperously during the sit-in, this does not mean that it was ineffective. Additional sit-ins will be required only if the problem behavior remains as it was after the sit-in is over.

BREAKING THE SEAL OF SECRECY: ENLISTING SUPPORTERS, MEDIATORS, AND PUBLIC OPINION

Involving other people in what is happening at home is a major factor in coping with the child's extreme behaviors by nonviolent resistance. Secrecy is one of the chief characteristics of families with domestic violence. Experience shows that so long as secrecy is maintained, the violence continues. Many parents feel the need to keep the problems secret so as to protect the family name and to avoid stigmatizing the child. This, however, may cut the family from all sources of support, leaving it unprotected and isolated. Remember: Breaking the seal of secrecy and enlisting support from outsiders is the first step in stopping the violence.

Turning to friends and relatives and letting them into the secret is not an easy decision. You may have to overcome serious inhibitions to be able to perform this step. However, when you find the courage to do so, you will see that people react positively to your request for help and that your child will be affected by the support you get. Your sense of personal worth and the security of your family will grow. The people you enlist may help in various ways: by being a source of confirmation and encouragement to you, by subjecting the violent child to the pressure of public opinion, by giving practical help, and by serving as mediators.

Ask the people you informed to make contact with the child in person or by phone, letter, e-mail, or fax. It is helpful to give these people a copy of these instructions. Ask them to tell your child that her extreme behavior is totally unacceptable. In cases where violence (toward you, siblings, or property) occurs, they should tell the child that her acts can be defined as "domestic violence" and are a criminal offense. They should tell her that they are determined to help you stop the violence.

These overtures will make it clear to the child that what she does is no longer done in private but that people know about the home situation and are ready to help you. Don't forget that the use of the written word has a power of its own. If you have relatives or friends who live faraway to whom the child is attached, phone calls, faxes, and letters from them can have a strong impact. By these measures, the child will understand that you are no longer alone. In many cases this knowledge is enough to significantly diminish the violence.

The inclusion of third parties from outside the family opens up additional opportunities. One of these is mediation. In most cases, someone will be found among friends and relatives who can develop a good contact with the child. This person can suggest compromises that might well be rejected if they came directly from you. The mediator can help convince the child to retreat from extreme positions (e.g., to return home after he has left in protest). The mediator also contributes by lessening the child's isolation in the new situation. Especially in crises (when, e.g., the child closes himself off, breaks off contact, or runs away), involving a mediator is a crucial means to lessen escalation. In another section we meet another group of people who can act as mediators: the child's friends and their parents.

THE TELEPHONE ROUND

The telephone round is a way of manifesting parental presence and nonviolent resistance when the child comes home at late hours, refuses to tell you where he spends his time, or runs away from home. The telephone round consists in the systematic contacting of a whole list of people to whom the child is connected. The procedure has a number of objectives:

1. manifesting parental presence and reasserting your right to supervise the child

2. finding the child

3. exerting collective pressure on the child to return home, and

4. returning the child to the home.

As can be seen from the order of the objectives, returning the child home is not the primary goal. The most important goal is to reaffirm your right and ability to be present and to supervise. The telephone round achieves this goal, even if you do not locate the child, because you will be leaving your mark on many areas of the child's life (every phone call conveys the message: "We are here!"). Therefore, even if the child does not immediately return home, you have succeeded in showing parental presence, in manifesting nonviolent resistance toward the child's disappearance, and in widening your support net.

The telephone round makes it clear that you have decided to break the seal of secrecy and emerge from isolation. By getting in touch with various people and showing your parental concern, you will be publicizing the objective and the nonviolent nature of your struggle. Don't be surprised if other parents who are in the same situation as you show a warm interest.

Collecting Information

You begin by finding out the phone numbers and addresses of as many of the child's friends, acquaintances, and places of entertainment she frequents as possible. This may be achieved by looking at school lists, asking the child's friends for their phone numbers, or, in cases when you are worried that the child is involved in illegal activities, by getting the numbers stored in the child's cellular phone. You may rightly wonder whether some of these procedures are not excessively invasive. Your guiding rule should then be how much you feel your child is in danger. The greater this danger, the more you may feel justified in intruding into the child's privacy.

Making the Calls

The telephone round consists in calling systematically the people and places on your list. It is important to phone many numbers on the list and not only the place where you think the child is, since you not only want to locate her, but also to convey a message of parental presence. Phoning the child's cellular phone directly does not really help. On the contrary, by restricting yourself to such a direct call, you are as much as declaring that you are not yet ready to resist.

If the hour is late, it may not be advisable to conduct the round at this time. You can then postpone it until the next evening. If the child protests that she was already at home and that there was no reason to embarrass her by calling her friends, you may answer that you are not ready to remain unable to know where she was the night before.

Talking to the Child's Friends

Introduce yourself, say that your child has not come home, that you are very worried, and that you are looking for her. Ask whether the friend has seen her at school, has heard about her plans, or has any idea where she might be. Ask the friend to tell your child that you are worried and looking for her. Ask him whether he can try and convince her to get in contact with you. If it seems that the friend is willing to help you, it is worthwhile arranging a meeting with him. Your support network will then include some of your child's friends. These friends may serve as mediators, helping to reduce escalation at crucial junctures. Even if the friend is not cooperative, there is a good chance that he will tell your child that you called, even if only for the pleasure to have a jibe at her. Your goal is not the jibe, but the manifestation of presence. In the friend's message to your child, you have left the clear sign "We were here!" At the end of the conversation with the friend, ask him to call one of his parents to the phone.

Talking to the Friends' Parents

Introduce yourself, ask them whether they have seen your child lately, and ask them not to let your child stay overnight in their house without your express permission. At times, you will find out that the friend's parents react warmly and interestedly. In this case, it is worthwhile arranging a meeting with them. Parental networks created in this way have great potential. These parents may also serve as mediators sometimes. They are particularly helpful in getting information, in case your child runs away from home. For they can then address their own child and say to him: "Now it is no joke! She has run away! You must help me help her parents find her!" Children thus addressed often cooperate.

Talking to Owners of Places of Entertainment and Their Workers
You can ask them to try and locate your child in their establishment and tell her that you are looking for her.

There is a chance that in the course of the telephone round you will locate your child. This will open up the option for another intervention: tailing.

TAILING

Tailing is a parental activity the aim of which is to reestablish contact when your child attempts to eschew parental supervision or run away. Tailing is geared both to prevent the damage caused by questionable activities taking place away from parental supervision and to counter the cut-off process that your child initiated. Thus, instead of reacting to the child's attempt to break off contact with an escalation of the cut-off process (e.g., by locking the door of the house or stopping to talk to the child), tailing shows the parents' determination to maintain contact and remain present.

As with other measures of nonviolent resistance, the child will try to bring the parental action to a stop. These reactions are mainly of two types: an attempt to create conflict and an attempt to deepen the cut-off. To counter these reactions, hold steadily to the decision to withstand all provocations and try as much as you can to maintain contact and supervision. Keep repeating to yourselves: "We will not be provoked and will not give in!"

Tailing can be an appropriate response in the following cases.

1. *The child runs away from home.* Children who run away usually try to find refuge with a friend or relative. Alternatively, they may join a group of youngsters who live marginally. Although running

away is an extreme act, the child is likely not to be surprised by your arrival; he knows that you may react unusually to an unusual event.

2. *The child does not come home at night when he was supposed to or disappears for long periods during the day.* Unlike running away from home, which is an extraordinary event and indicates a particularly stormy situation, late returns and daily disappearances tend to be routine occurrences. Children often view these disappearances as their "basic right," a view that is reinforced by the parents' long-standing inability to prevent them. So, although daily disappearances are less extreme than running away, the child is liable to be shocked by the parents' arrival and react with greater intensity.

3. *The child keeps bad company.* Bad company is one of the surest predictors of deterioration. Unsupervised time spent in such company can put the child at risk of using drugs, dropping out of school, or engaging in delinquent behavior.

The following are a number of principles to guide your behavior when you find the child.

1. Ask her to come home with you and state that you will not punish her.

2. Avoid arguments. If possible, keep silent for as long as you remain with the child at his runaway place.

3. Avoid any act that could lead to escalation (e.g., taking hold of the child by force and putting him in the car).

4. Tail the child for as long as possible.

Remember: The success of the intervention lies not in returning the child home but in demonstrating parental presence and in reaffirming your decision to supervise the child's doings.

Tailing When the Child Is at a Friend's House

Ring the bell and say that you have come to take your child home. Say that you have no intention of punishing the child, but that you want him to come with you. If you get an evasive answer, or if the child refuses to come to the door, say that you will wait for him. You can ask the friend or his parents to wait inside. If you are not invited to come in, ring the bell again every ten minutes and ask the child to come home with you.

Tailing When the Child Is at a Street Corner, a Party, or a Club

Approach the child and say you want him to come home with you and that he will not be punished. If he runs away (a typical reaction), do not run after him. Instead, take the opportunity to make contact with his friends. Introduce yourselves, ask them their names and telephone numbers (children will often give you the number if you say it is only for urgent situations), and explain why you are concerned about your child. If you feel this is irrelevant, for this is exactly the "bad company" your child is frequenting, remember that these kids are not all the same. Some of them are not all "bad company" and may be of much help in some circumstances. If the kids say that you should not worry, for all of them do the same and nothing really bad is happening, you may answer: "I know my child well, and I know she doesn't have much self-control. Maybe you have more self-control than she." Interestingly, most kids will agree to this judgment (most of them believe they have more self-control than others). Or if your child is younger than the others, you might say: "It could be that you are more mature. My daughter is only fourteen!" This conversation may enlist some unexpected supporters for your cause. Some of these children may play an all-important role as mediators. In a number of the cases we treated, friends who were enlisted in this way helped to return a runaway child home.

Tailing When the Child Has Run Away from Home and Joined a Group of Other Marginal Youngsters

In these cases, you should be prepared to tail the child for an extended time. In one of our cases, the parents sat for three days near the beach where the youngsters were living until their daughter (who had already been away from home a whole month) decided to come home with them.

In all of the above situations, it might be worthwhile taking a friend or relative along. Tailing takes considerable courage and you will need all the support you can get. The presence of a third party at your side can also be of significance in reducing the risk of escalation (the child will behave less extremely if you have somebody with you). The third party may also be able to mediate: the child will accept a proposal coming from them better than one that came from you.

THE PROTRACTED SIT-DOWN STRIKE

In distinction from the sit-in, the protracted sit-down strike takes a few days (usually three), is made in the presence of as many supporters as possible, and takes place throughout the house.

The sit-down strike is indicated in the wake of a particularly acute event, such as when the child is brought home after running away, hits the parent for the first time, or gets caught by the police in criminal activities.

The sit-down strike is structured as a rite of passage, that is, an event that indicates life is at a turning point so that the situation after the ceremony is different from that before it. The rite is an event of symbolic and practical significance. Parents, relatives, and friends often feel and react differently to the child's negative behaviors after the strike.

Preparations for the sit-down strike include the following:

1. *Freeing yourself from all other commitments (including work).*

2. *Getting the participation of as many friends, relatives, and people who are acquainted with the child (e.g., teachers, youth group leaders, the child's friends and their parents, and your own friends and relatives) as possible.* A possible form for such an invitation could be: "We appeal to you for help regarding something unfortunate that took place this week (give a detailed description of what happened). As a result of this, we are sitting at home for three days and inviting friends, relatives, and people who care for our child to come and visit us and help

us find a solution. Your attendance is extremely important to us!"
If doubts concerning the sit-down strike are expressed by some of
the people who are being invited, you can say: "We are doing this
because we are afraid of losing our child. We are trying to come up
with ideas and get help before it is too late!" By their participation,
the people who come in become witnesses and help validate the
event, thus reinforcing the message that things cannot continue the
way they are. The guests can also raise practical suggestions and help
by mediating. Some of the guests may be asked whether they would
be willing to give practical help (e.g., with homework, helping find
work for a youngster, or offering him emotional support). It is a good
idea for friends and relatives to bring food for the family or cook for
them in their home. Bringing and preparing food is one of the most
basic ways of expressing support. People who cannot come can be
asked to express their support by speaking with the parents and the
child by phone or by sending the child a fax. In this way relatives
and friends who live far away also can participate.

3. *Preparing the house: the key from the door to the child's room should
be taken out, food should be prepared for three days, arrangements should
be made to receive the guests, and plans should be made to stop the child
from running away.*

A crucial element of the sit-down strike is maximum public exposure. The extreme event that led to the sit-down strike provides the
justification for the far-reaching breach in long-standing habits of
secrecy. This breach constitutes a deep change in life conditions and
thus contributes to the effectiveness of the strike as a rite of passage.
The breach of secrecy will have a deep impact not only on the child
but on you as well.

The event is launched when the child and a few helpers (two or
three) are present. It is a good idea to have one of the child's friends
present, too. The friend's presence helps minimize the polarization
that could develop if only people whom the child identifies with
you were in the house. The event opens with your announcement:
"We have decided to hold a sit-down strike for three days, so that
we can find a solution to the situation that was created because of

the unfortunate event that happened this week (describe what happened). During these days we will all be home and will receive visits from various people who will come to help us. We will not work and we will not go out. You (the child) will stay home with us. You will not be scolded or punished. We are not interested in punishing you. This is not our goal. Our goal is to find a way for our family to get out of this difficult situation." If this message cannot be conveyed directly, ask a mediator to pass it on to the child.

As in the sit-in, you should resist the child's attempt to leave the house by standing in front of the door. If the child manages to get out, the sit-down strike continues, including a massive telephone round. If the child is located, a transition can be made to tailing (by one of the parents who is accompanied by at least one of the helpers). In the case of a single parent, it is desirable for at least one of the supporters to stay home and continue sitting with the guests. If the child refuses to talk to the family or the visitors, the sit-down strike continues as planned, with visitors greeting her when they arrive and saying goodbye when they leave and leaving her written messages. It is a good idea for the guests to leave the child small, symbolic presents (such as greeting cards, flowers, or candy). There should be no attempt to make contact with the child against her will. If the child accuses you of coercion, violence, humiliation, or betrayal, you should answer (personally or through mediators): "We have no intention of humiliating you. We also have no interest in subjugating you. We are acting as we are because we cannot continue to live with the situation that has been created." Visitors should express support for the parents' announcement as simply and concisely as possible. If the child is prepared to make contact with only a few people or even one person, these persons should act as mediators. The mediator should try and bridge the gap between child and parents without blaming either side. Any suggestions raised by the mediator should be discussed by you and your supporters and, if the child agrees, by her and anyone she may trust.

At the end of the event, there should be no threats or warnings of any kind. The event should be summed up in writing and the

summary sent to all the participants. This summary is not a contract the child must sign but a description of the rite of passage. The
visitors are asked to continue phoning the family and the child in
the days and weeks after the strike. It would be a mistake to think
that after a big event such as a sit-down strike, one should invariably
react massively every time the child behaved badly. The response
to such incidents should be the more usual steps of nonviolent resistance. However, the sit-down strike will now allow you to follow these steps more consequently and with a higher degree of
support.

"REFUSING ORDERS"

"Refusing orders" is a measure of nonviolent resistance in which you
(1) stop performing those activities that you feel forced to perform
and (2) go back to performing those activities that you feel were
forbidden to you. "Refusing orders" has a number of objectives:

1. to counter your habits of automatic obedience

2. to sharpen your awareness of the many services you feel obliged
to provide, and

3. to increase your freedom.

While sit-ins, telephone rounds, and sit-down strikes are meant to
provide a suitable answer to unusual occurrences, "refusing orders"
provides an answer for routine situations (such as driving the child
everywhere or serving food at the exact moment and in the exact
way it is demanded). "Refusing orders" is meant to disturb a status
quo that has become unbearable.

We can assume that this status quo developed over the years,
in a gradual and almost imperceptible process. Little by little, you
"learned" to act in accordance with the child's every whim. In this
process, your freedom shrunk while the child's power grew unabat-
edly. The more obedient you became to his wishes, the less consid-
erate he became toward yours. When you begin to "refuse orders,"

you will discover that this state of affairs cannot exist without your consent. You will become aware that your consent is not freely given but is the result of the child's coercive acts and explicit or implicit threats. Your objective in "refusing orders" is not to punish the child but to put a stop to your own submissive behavior and to recover your personal and parental voice.

"Refusing orders" can be conducted on two planes.

1. *Refusing services*: stopping all unnecessary services that are extorted or taken for granted, and

2. *Breaking taboos*: engaging in activities that you avoid because of the child's veto.

Refusing Services

Begin by reviewing all the services you provide, and ask yourself which ones you perform out of your own free will and which ones under duress. As you will see, this review is not all easy, since the forms of coercion can be subtle and the habits of obedience so ingrained that the services have become natural to you. Some examples of services that parents chose to refuse are: driving the children to afternoon activities, friends' houses, places of entertainment, private lessons, etc.; buying junk food or cooking or serving food in a particular manner; paying for expensive pastimes or fancy clothes; paying for cellular phones, Internet services, and cable TV service; or giving the child large amounts of money.

Refusing a service is not the same as administering a punishment. The two are different in their aims and processes, as well as in the messages they convey:

1. The refusal is not meant as a response to a particular negative behavior of the child but is a consequence of the parents' understanding that the services are the result of coercion. When you refuse a service, don't say: "So long as you behave like this, I won't do this!" Say, rather: "I found out that I feel bad performing this service, so I decided to stop it."

2. The services are not restored as a result of the child's "good behavior." However, the parents are free to restore some of the services if they are convinced that the child's threat and their own feeling of coercion have ceased to exist.

3. Punishment is meant to change the child, whereas refusing services is meant to change the parents (putting a stop to their automatic obedience). Of course, refusing services is also likely to improve the child's behavior, but this achievement is secondary to the change in parental presence and self-esteem.

Breaking Taboos

Begin by reviewing the areas in the house and your life at large in which there is a ban on your freedom of action. Some typical bans are: not being allowed to enter the child's room, being forbidden to invite guests, being limited in the cleaning or arrangement of the house, not being able to watch television in the living room, not being allowed to speak freely on the phone, being forbidden to ask questions about the child's school or friends, or being forbidden to address these friends. Probably over the years, friends and relatives have already remarked that you accept the child's bans without flinching. It is often in these areas or in areas you feel afraid that others might notice that it may be most worthwhile breaking the taboo. After you decide which bans you want to focus on, gather support from friends or relatives or even from those people who first directed your attention to the matter.

You can expect the child to react to your attempt to break taboos by threats, violence, or sweeping accusations. React by following strictly the principles of nonviolent resistance: do not give in and withstand all provocations. You can respond to the child's attempts to make you overturn your decision by calling in your support system and by reacting with any appropriate nonviolent strategy (sit-ins, telephone rounds, tailing, mobilizing public opinion, etc.).

When you begin "refusing orders," announce your decision quietly and with no hint of a threat or indication of "I'm the boss!" Don't provide unnecessary explanations, don't justify yourself, and don't argue. All of these will lead to escalation.

"Refusing orders" may quickly and significantly improve your self-esteem. Parents often say they have found themselves again. After your ability to "refuse orders" has become clearly established, you may reconsider whether you would desire to restore some of the interrupted services. It is then important to ask yourselves: "Am I sure I am no longer feeling threatened or coerced?" "Do I want to restore the service?" "Do I feel free to deny giving the service again, if I want to or if circumstances change?" In all of these questions you are the focus of the inquiry, not the child. Restoring services, like refusing them, depends on you and is aimed at improving your feelings as a parent and as a human being.

RECONCILIATION GESTURES

Reconciliation gestures help to broaden your relationship with your child, so that it is no longer limited to the conflict between you and your child. Research on escalation shows that the performance of such gestures reduces mutual aggression and improves the relationship. Reconciliation gestures are not a prize, and they do not depend on the child's behavior. They allow you to express your love, while simultaneously carrying out nonviolent resistance. Reconciliation gestures do not replace nonviolent resistance but run parallel to it.

The following are some main types of reconciliation gestures.

1. *Statements, verbal or written, that express esteem and respect for the child, her talents, and her qualities.* You can also express respect for her determination and even for her fighting spirit. Don't fear that this would strengthen the child in her fight against you; on the contrary, by giving this quality express recognition, you partly obviate the child's need to demonstrate it.

2. *Treats, such as food the child is especially fond of, or symbolic presents.* It is important to be prepared for the child's refusal to accept the treat. In such a case, limit yourself to saying that you prepared the treat for her, but that she is free to take it or leave it. Treats should have no strings attached: the child decides how and whether to accept them. Treats should never be expensive gifts (such as a trip abroad) or something the child demands as a condition for improving his behavior. One treat with a special positive significance is to fix any of the child's belongings that the child broke in a fit of rage. Fixing the object then becomes symbolic for the desire to repair the relationship. Don't be afraid that the child will view you as weak. Your objective is not to look strong but to demonstrate parental presence. Treats are a way to do so in a pleasant manner.

3. *Suggesting a shared activity.* You could suggest going on a hike, seeing a film, or participating in another shared activity that the child likes and was perhaps used to doing with you in the past. Remember that she has the right to refuse without this being held against her.

4. *A special type of reconciliation gesture is expressing regret for your own violent reactions in the past.* Some parents have reservations about this, fearing to be viewed as weak. Remember that reconciliation gestures are performed in parallel to nonviolent resistance. For this reason, a reconciliation gesture is never a token of submission but a positive gesture made out of choice.

It is very likely that at first the child will reject your reconciliation gestures. This may simply indicate that your child is used to rejecting all your proposals indiscriminately or that she may fear that by accepting them she will appear weak. Reconciliation gestures, however, have importance even when they are rejected, since they begin to restore parental presence in a positive way. Continue therefore with reconciliation gestures without forcing them on the child. In some cases, the child declares his rejection, while silently giving a token of acceptance. For instance, a child may refuse something the mother cooked for him, but the food item disappears from the fridge during the night. "Officially," the child has refused, but the food is already in his stomach, doing some productive parental work in there.

CONCLUSION

The means of nonviolent resistance that we have detailed afford you considerable power. This is not the power to subdue but the power to resist and to recover your voice as persons and parents. The depth and extent of this power can be best understood when you consider that this is not just a collection of techniques but a series of interrelated measures that stem from a unified concept and that mutually reinforce one another. Thus nonviolent resistance does not come into being automatically as you hold a sit-in or perform a telephone round. The effect of the process is cumulative and lies in the inner connections between the methods, the messages, and the attitudes it engenders. The following is a short review of some of the links in this chain:

You announce your decision not to continue living with the present situation.

You break the seal of silence and enlist support.

You ask the supporters to announce to the child that they know about his behavior.

You perform sit-ins, telephone rounds, tailing, and sit-down strikes with the appropriate support and according to need.

You enlist supporters among the child's friends and their parents.

You encourage mediators to step in.

You free yourselves from habits of automatic obedience by refusing services exacted by threats and by breaking taboos.

You make reconciliation gestures.

You do not give in.

You withstand provocations.

These activities reinforce one another. Your willingness to devote yourself to the task will make it clear to the child and to yourself that the situation has changed irrevocably.

Preparing for the task demands commitment and responsibility. To ensure success, you must give nonviolent resistance the highest priority. From our experience, you must remain in a state of high commitment for a period of about three months. After this period, the former situation will not return. The feeling of concentrated effort that you will experience will gradually lessen, since during this period you will develop new habits. Gradually, you will overcome your tendency to give in and your high reactivity to provocations. Even if your child attempts to revert to those means she employed in the past, she will no longer meet with similar reactions from you. This will lead to a deeper change in the home atmosphere and in the relationship between you and your child.

To achieve this change, it is essential not to fall into the illusion of immediate results. Parents who expect that after one or two sit-ins the child will totally change his behavior are in for a disappointment. We generally tell parents that even after they have invested some fifteen hours of concentrated display of parental presence (performing sit-ins, telephone rounds, enlisting support, making reconciliation gestures, etc.), they still will have not reached the desired commitment level. But after this initial investment, you will begin seeing signs of adjustment in your child. At times you may have doubts whether the change in the child is deep enough. These doubts are both justified and useful: they keep you from becoming complacent. Actually, the real change is taking place in you. It is you who are learning to act, think, and feel differently! As you gradually become a more experienced practitioner of nonviolent resistance, the less will be the destructive potential of your child's and of your own acts.

In this tempering process you must ready yourself for the child's reactions. Be sure that she will not easily give up the power to which she has become accustomed. On the contrary, she will try to the best of her ability to convince you that your efforts are not only futile but also damaging. She will try to get you to submit again or to provoke you into uncontrollable reactions. Keep in mind that submission and hostile confrontations are a serious setback. You must especially be wary of the danger of being provoked into violence. Any such outburst on your part is sure to require lengthy repair work. Your child will surely employ such means as have worked in the past: if she used to frighten you with dire threats, to provoke you into endless arguing, to make you lose control by insulting remarks, to make you pity her, or to drive you into endless worrying, she is likely to do this again. The following principles may help you cope with these reactions.

The child's reactions are mostly attempts to make you give in or lose control. Being prepared, refusing to give in, and withstanding provocations will take the edge off the child's acute reactions. Remember: If you do not give in or lose control, the process of escalation runs out of fuel.

Harsh reactions pass quickly. You must not think that the child is capable of keeping up his extreme behavior for long stretches of time; the harsher the reaction, the shorter its duration.

Use the support of others to withstand the child's harsh reactions. Calling in your helpers and supporters will increase your endurance and help to give the child the message that you are not alone and are not about to give in.

Above all, remember: Parental presence and nonviolent resistance are the best safeguards against the child's violent and self-destructive acts.

4 NONVIOLENT RESISTANCE IN ACTION

Before examining case examples of nonviolent resistance, we must first deal with some common assumptions that contribute much to parental ineffectiveness. Although these assumptions have often been dealt with in the literature, they are still quite prevalent. We thus feel the need to clear the field once more.

Aggressive behaviors are only "symptoms" of deeper psychological problems. This assumption may weaken the parents' determination to resist the child's negative behaviors, for dealing with mere "symptoms" may be not only useless, but also harmful. Dozens of studies have relegated this belief to the realm of superstition by showing that treating "symptoms" does not cause the situation to get worse or lead to the appearance of new ones. In fact, quite the opposite is the case: directly treating negative behaviors commonly leads not only to local but also to more generalized improvements. This phenomenon is called the "ripple effect": parents who used a consistent restraining policy to stop the child's damaging behaviors not only reduced these behaviors, but also improved the child's functioning in other areas over time. Conversely, opting for a permissive and acceptant approach toward these behaviors led to their worsening and to a more negative prognosis over time (Bates et al. 1998; Baumrind 1971, 1991; Chamberlain & Patterson 1995; Eisenberg & Murphy 1995; Florsheim, Tolan, & Gorman-Smith 1998; Hetherington, Cox, & Cox 1975; Patterson et al. 1992).

The best answer to the child's aggressive behaviors is individual psychotherapy. Following this assumption, the parents of a child who, for instance, is caught stealing or behaves violently often decide to send her to individual therapy. Sometimes, when the child is violent at school, the school may even make this a condition for the child's staying in school. Such decisions are almost always mistaken. First, the referral conveys the message that the child is not responsible for her behavior. Further, the referral creates the illusion the negative behavior is now being properly dealt with. Moreover, if the child agrees to go to therapy under such circumstances, it is usually only to avoid disciplinary measures. This is a sure way to discourage positive motivation. No wonder that the most extensive study to date on the effect of individual psychotherapy (as the exclusive treatment modality) on delinquent children found that the child's delinquent behavior and the parents' helplessness increased (Borduin et al. 1995). Individual therapy can surely be of help to children with a wide range of psychological problems, but only if it is not imposed or undergone for ulterior motives.

All the child needs is acceptance, warmth, and freedom from hampering demands. According to the permissive ideology, children thus raised would grow up as loving, creative, and secure human beings. This belief extends itself also to the curative properties of the ideally permissive and accepting environment. Thus the parents of aggressive children who apply for professional help are often told that all they have to do is give their child more love and acceptance. This therapeutic attitude can be doubly harmful, for it increases the parents' sense of guilt and helplessness and fosters a parental attitude that may actually worsen the problem behaviors. Baumrind's classic studies (1971, 1991) showed that a permissive home ideology leads to an increase in a host of behavioral problems (such as school drop-out, violence, drug abuse, and delinquency). These findings were confirmed by dozens of investigations (for a summary of the findings, see Chamberlain & Patterson 1995; Eisenberg & Murphy 1995).

The sanctity of privacy. The right to privacy has a very high place in the value scale of Western society. Parents often shrink from procedures they view as invasive, such as supervising the child or entering his room, even when they have ample evidence that the child is involved in dangerous activities. The sanctity of privacy is upheld by the very structure of individual psychotherapy: thus even with small children, parents must unconditionally accept that all therapeutic matters are out of bounds for them. Any attempt on their part to be informed about what goes on behind the closed door of the therapy room may be interpreted as a lack of respect for the child's individuality. Privacy, however, is only one value among others. When conflict arises between privacy and other values, such as the need to guarantee the child's safety, one must weigh the cost of unconditionally opting for privacy. Research shows that parental supervision (which limits the child's privacy) reduces children's antisocial and risky behaviors, whereas parental inability or unwillingness to supervise increases them (Frick et al. 1992; Funk 1996; Kolvin et al. 1988; Laub & Simpson 1988; Loeber & Dishion 1984; Loeber & Stouthamer-Loeber 1986; Wilson 1987). Parental knowledge of the child's whereabouts has been shown to reduce the child's vulnerability to negative social pressure (Steinberg 1986). This finding clarifies how parental presence exerts its influence: children whose parents make sure to know exactly where they spend their time feel that the parents are present even when they are physically distant. Our intention, however, is not to turn parental supervision into an absolute value. With a dependent or insecure child who does not exhibit any violent or risky behaviors, it might be advisable to minimize parental supervision.

When persuasion fails, force will do the job. This belief underlies all parental attempts to restore the parents' authority by shouting, threats, harsh punishments, and beatings. Presumably, this show of force would restore the family hierarchy to its right form, with the parents undisputedly at the top. This attitude has many supporters, even among professionals. One of its chief dangers is a rapid escalation, for many children will respond in kind. Alternatively, when the sides fail to bring each other into unconditional surrender, they may opt for cutting off the relationship. The most common variety of cutoff is that between the father and the child. The damage may then also extend to the marital relationship: the father, for example, may say that, due to the mother's leniency, he is prevented from educating the child and is therefore forced to leave the field. The father's retreat further worsens the situation, for it weakens the parental presence even more. Nonviolent resistance offers a clear alternative to this vicious cycle. The goal of nonviolent resistance is not to subjugate the child but to restore parental presence. The opposition between the "tough" and the "soft" parental stances gives way to a synthesis: the parents no longer "impose limits" by means of punishment inflicted from above, but instead set limits to the child's destructive behavior through their determined and caring personal presence.

CASE 1: THE TORNADO

Rebecca and Michael came to us for counseling as the last resort before deciding to hospitalize their thirteen-year-old son, Ron. The psychiatrist in charge of the case was convinced that Ron presented a real danger to his mother and siblings. He viewed the hospitalization as an interim stage that would prepare the way for Ron's removal from his home.

Ron had been diagnosed in kindergarten as suffering from attention-deficit disorder and hyperactivity. He was then described by his teacher as extremely impulsive and violent. Various medical treatments had been tried, with no effect. In addition, the family had attended family therapy for many months, and Ron had been in individual therapy for over a year. In spite of all this, the situation seemed to be worsening.

Ron's behavior at home kept Rebecca in a state of constant anxiety. She compared him to a tornado: he would threaten, scream, curse, throw things about, and strike out whenever his demands were not immediately met. For example, if the food was not on the table at the moment and in the manner he demanded, a severe outburst would follow. His younger sister (seven years old) was his chief victim: Ron called her "retarded" and "mongoloid" and hit her several times a day, sometimes with a stick or a plate. Ron's ten-year-old brother also got his share of blows. Ron would not let them use the computer when he was at home, even if he wasn't using it at the time. He turned their rooms upside-down when their friends were there, and as a result they had stopped inviting friends. The parents could not leave the children alone for fear that Ron would do them serious harm. Rebecca was also a frequent target of Ron's violence, especially if she tried to protect the other children. In effect, her attempts to intervene in this area often enlarged the conflict: Ron would hit or humiliate his brother or sister, Rebecca would shout at him, he would swear at her, she would threaten punishment, he would shove or spit at her, she would announce a harsh punishment, and he would usually throw himself upon her, kicking, punching, and biting. After such a battle, Ron would become conciliatory and ask whiningly to make up with her. Rebecca, however, would feel her affection blocked.

When the father was around, the situation was somewhat better: Michael often managed to calm or control Ron, sometimes by actual bribery and sometimes by a show of force. Michael still had occasional good moments with Ron, such as going to the movies or playing soccer in the park. Sometimes Ron would spend a quiet hour in Michael's office at the end of the school day.

Surprisingly, at school, where Ron studied in a small class for children with attention-deficit disorders, there were no special complaints about him. The parents didn't know how to explain the difference between school and home. They noticed, however, that at home Ron controlled himself better when other adults were present. As the therapist focused on these situations, Rebecca and Michael agreed that Ron was not totally unable to control his behavior.

Ron's social situation was very bad. In the past he had had contact with other children, although mostly short-lived. Often these contacts would blow up after the first or second meeting, when Ron felt that things were not going his way. In the last year, all contacts had stopped. Nobody visited him at home, nobody called, nor did he call or visit others.

When Rebecca was asked whether she had any pleasant times with Ron, her eyes filled with tears, and she said she had not experienced any such moments for a long time. She felt that the constant frustration, anxiety, and anger were wiping out all feelings of caring and pleasure. She was glad that Michael still had good moments with Ron. When asked whether she could imagine such a possibility for her, she said, crying: "I no longer feel that I love him at all!"

We decided to place our emphasis on the following ingredients of nonviolent resistance: (1) withstanding provocations and delaying all disciplinary acts to a calmer time, (2) holding sit-ins, (3) enlisting support and public opinion (thus relying on Ron's tendency to respond favorably to outside people), and (4) making reconciliation gestures. The parents quickly learned to describe their present behaviors and past mistakes in the terms of parental presence and nonviolent resistance. They understood that their aim was not to subdue Ron but to restore their presence and protect the family against his violence.

In the beginning, Michael and Rebecca found it very hard to share their difficulties with outside people. The value they put on their own and on Ron's privacy stood in the way of their effectively breaking the cover of secrecy. The therapist expressed her understanding for this parental attitude, but clarified that so long as they remained alone with the problem, the violence might be perpetuated. Michael, in particular, could not accept this verdict. They chose therefore to begin by implementing only the other parts of the program.

The first sit-in was performed the very next day after the beginning of the therapy. Ron had badly attacked and humiliated his sister. Although the parents had expected violence on Ron's part during the sit-in, they chose not to involve a third party. As anticipated, Ron became wild and Michael had to hold him by force for the whole hour. The parents finished the sit-in exhausted and filled with doubts about the appropriateness of the program for their case. However, after an additional therapy session, they decided to give nonviolent resistance a more patient and systematic trial. They also agreed they had no choice but to involve other people.

They told their story and described the program to Rebecca's parents and to a friend of Michael's at work. The grandparents and the friend made contact with Ron and declared their intention to support the parents in their struggle against violence. From this moment on, Michael and Rebecca conducted sit-ins with one or two additional people present. In parallel, they began searching for possible reconciliation gestures. Rebecca had been used to hugging Ron before bedtime until a year before. This way of expressing affection had succumbed to the violent atmosphere. Rebecca hesitated to start hugging Ron again, claiming that "he didn't deserve a prize for his behavior." The therapist explained that reconciliation gestures were not prizes, but ways of broadening the relationship and preventing escalation. The therapist added that Rebecca's difficulty in hugging Ron was perfectly understandable, particularly so long as she felt she was a helpless victim of Ron's violence. By entering the program of nonviolent resistance, however, she would be getting out of her passive helplessness and this might bring a change in her ability to experience more positive emotions. Rebecca decided to try. She went back to hugging and kissing Ron before bedtime, regardless of his behavior during the day. Later in the treatment, she told the therapist that she felt wonderful about having restored this custom.

Michael and Rebecca's adherence to the principle of withstanding provocations led to a considerable reduction in the escalation cycles. The very knowledge that they could respond to Ron's outbursts later in the day (either by sit-ins or by asking other people to call Ron or send him a fax) contributed to their feeling of competence. This feeling began to express itself also in Rebecca's relationship with her other children. She told the therapist that she had a feeling she was talking differently to them, as if she had stopped being taken for granted.

The combination of reconciliation measures with nonviolent resistance gradually began bearing fruit. The outbursts diminished. Manifestations of spontaneous caring began to appear between Ron and Rebecca. Ron apologized more frequently for his violent episodes and Rebecca felt more able to accept his apologies, viewing them as an indication that his positive internal voices were growing stronger.

Michael and Rebecca not only did not go back on their decision to involve other people, but actually decided to broaden the net. They told a number of friends about the program and invited them home.

One of these new helpers left Ron a message expressing her respect for his achievements in self-control and saying she was quite sure that in the future his strength and power would bring him many positive achievements. Ron's behavior improved further, as the parents' support net widened. Physical violence during the sit-ins ceased entirely. Ron would still shout and swear, but would apologize for doing so immediately after the sit-in and control himself in the days that followed. The parents told the therapist that the inclusion of outside helpers had brought about the most significant change.

Six weeks after the beginning of the therapy, the parents were able to report a significant change in their own behavior. Rebecca felt she had much reduced her shouting, threatening, and incessant talking, while Michael had stopped buying quiet by means of bribes. The cooperation between them improved and they developed the ability to signal each other when one of them was in danger of getting involved in escalation.

The changes in Ron's violent behavior were gradual but far-reaching. At first, the physical violence lessened, then violence toward objects. In the last two weeks of the two-month therapy there was not a single case of physical violence of any kind. The positive moments increased, and Ron even began showing warmth and caring toward his brother and sister. All in all, his relationship toward his siblings remained rather gruff, but the hitting and the humiliation disappeared. He still swore and shouted at moments of frustration, but with far less frequency and intensity.

With the change at home, improvements in Ron's social life also became manifest. He began bringing friends home and playing with children his own age. He went out with friends on a Saturday evening for the first time. The parents were very surprised by these changes, since they had made no efforts at all in this direction.

The hospitalization idea dropped from the family agenda. The parents went back to going out in the evening, and the younger siblings began inviting friends home once again. Despite this, the parents were still doubtful about the stability of the achievements. This is, of course, not surprising. The parents were encouraged when the therapist told them that the doubts were not only justified but useful, as it would help them to stay prepared.

CASE 2: WHO CHANGES, THE CHILD OR THE PARENT?

Clara was a divorced woman who, due to the father's having cut himself off from the family, functioned as a single parent to Alex and Jerry (twelve and seven years old). Clara expressed doubts about whether her coming to therapy was at all justified: Alex was indeed a difficult child, but maybe no more than many other children. What worried her most was Alex's "delinquent language." When asked for examples, all she could remember were expressions such as "Get out of here!" or "I'm sick of you!" Clara said Alex had been in individual therapy in the past for more than a year without any improvement, and, as for her, the meetings with Alex's therapist had been far from helpful: she felt that the therapist blamed her for Alex's problems.

Clara was surprised to discover that, in the present therapy, she was not being viewed as the source of Alex's problems. She was also surprised that the therapist was no less interested in her own pains than in Alex's mental condition. This understanding gradually helped disperse the fog that obscured her reports. She became more ready to share with the therapist some of Alex's "delinquent language," but, as if frightened about what she had just said, she would immediately ask herself whether he had really said those things. Or she would describe a severe incident, but immediately make the reservation that this was really not that important, for Alex had behaved reasonably for most of the day. Far from thinking that Clara was "showing resistance," the therapist thought she was struggling with all her might to stay afloat. Among the expressions she reported were, for instance: "If you don't do as I say right now, I'll kill you both tonight!" or "I'll stab you, you stinking whore!" or "It's nothing to me to finish you off and burn the house down." Or he would aim a toy pistol at his brother's head, pull the trigger and make an explosive sound, saying, "Too bad this isn't a real gun!" On one occasion, he pointed a sharp knife at his own chest, shouting hysterically, "I'm going to kill myself! I want to die!" Clara said that Alex's very tone of voice, even in the most trivial matters, conveyed a constant threat.

Clara also described situations in which Alex complained tearfully that she didn't love him and didn't care about him. Clara would then soothe and comfort him, making appeals that he change his behavior. Alex would then kiss her and ask her to hug him and kiss him back. Clara would do so. She said she had always been soft and sentimental, and, in these occasions, she often cried together with Alex. These close moments, however, had no effect on Alex's negative behavior.

Clara burst into tears when she described Alex's loneliness and suffering. She felt so overwhelmed by pity that she couldn't stop trying to compensate him, for instance, by buying him expensive treats. These attempts aroused fierce jealousy in Alex's brother. Jerry complained loudly that Alex not only hit him, but was also getting a prize for it!

Clara's main way to achieve some calm was to give in. She did this constantly, despite her clear understanding that, over time, things would not get any better. Lately, Alex had introduced a time dimension to his demands: "If you don't come and get me in five minutes, you'll see what will happen!" Alex was literally spelling down the principle of automatic obedience: Clara should be trained to react unflinchingly to his demands.

Without his acquaintance with the principles of nonviolent resistance, the therapist might have viewed Clara's automatic obedience as a sign of lacking motivation or even of masochistic submissiveness. In effect, many people would react to a story such as Clara's critically, claiming that she was actually "asking" for what she was getting. The principles of nonviolent resistance provide an antidote to such reactions: automatic obedience and the pessimistic belief that the situation cannot be changed are a *result* of violence and oppression, not their cause. This understanding allowed for the development of a solid therapeutic alliance with Clara, without which it would have been impossible to withstand the hardships ahead.

Preparations for action began with a shared reading of the "Guidelines for Parents." The illustrations to the different escalation processes were drawn from Clara's own interactions with Alex. Clara understood full well the importance of withstanding provocations, delaying her reactions, and enlisting support (she began by involving her brother, her sister, and two cousins). She quickly learned to differentiate between reconciliation gestures (which were made on her own initiative) and giving in to threat.

Clara's sister was present at the time of the first sit-in. Surprisingly, Alex acted cooperatively, although initially he made irrelevant suggestions, such as claiming that Clara was to blame for his own outbursts because she disturbed him while he was watching television, that Jerry was the one who always started the fights, and that the best solution was to send him (Alex) to a nuthouse. Clara answered curtly that these suggestions were not a solution. Gradually, Alex began talking more constructively. He suggested a day plan for sharing the computer, promised to stop using bad language, and asked Clara to "remind him" of this promise. Two hours after the sit-in, Alex knocked on his mother's bedroom door, and said that he was restraining himself so as not to fight with his brother. Clara phoned the therapist to report on these events. He found this a good beginning, but added that she should also be prepared for trouble.

After three days of very unusual quiet, Alex went back to threatening, shouting, and using abusive language. Clara reminded him of his promise, but Alex dismissed her reminder, adding a string of obscenities. This provoked Clara to threaten him back. She said she would sit in his room for days on end. This threat led to a bout of escalation, in which both Clara and Alex exchanged blows. On the wake of this crisis, Clara took it upon herself to scrupulously avoid such reactions in the future and adhere carefully to the principles of nonviolent resistance.

The second sit-in was carried out in the presence of Clara's brother and sister-in-law. Alex was less cooperative this time, suggesting only unacceptable solutions (e.g., that Clara hit him every time he swore or that she threaten him with extreme punishments). Clara was all the more surprised in that Alex behaved reasonably for more than a week following the sit-in. She remarked that Alex was becoming quiet and even sad. As is often the case with parents in such a situation, Clara began worrying about the change, asking herself whether Alex was not "losing the will to live." The therapist encouraged her, saying that Alex's sadness was understandable, showing he understood that he probably would have to relinquish some of his power.

The third sit-in was carried out as a result of Clara's being called to school. The teacher told her that Alex was talking a lot about drugs and sex and was caught surfing a pornographic site on the class computer. This time, although the reason for the sit-in was his behavior at school, Alex made some positive suggestions about his behavior at home. He suggested that he be allowed to be alone in the room he shared with his brother for half an hour every day, during which time he would be allowed to shout and curse as much as he wanted; as a result, he wouldn't "need" to curse outside. As for school, Alex agreed, for the first time, to get help with his studies. There followed a number of quiet days, which ended in what Clara described as a "catastrophe." For two full hours, Alex shouted, threatened, threw things about, and hit out indiscriminately. Clara lost all restraint, screaming and hitting back.

The crisis might have proved intractable were it not for Clara's good working alliance with the therapist. As it was, she did not despair, but asked him for close guidance on restoring nonviolent resistance. Clara's determination despite the setbacks was impressive. The following steps were decided on to improve Clara's self-control and intensify the nonviolent resistance.

1. Clara bought earplugs and put them in every time Alex began shouting. On these occasions she would say to Alex: "I'm putting in earplugs so as not to get angry; I am listening to you and can hear you, but less loudly!"

2. She appealed to six individuals whom Alex knew, asking them to call him by phone and send him letters in which they told him they were aware of what was going on. The terms "violence," "abuse," and "blackmail" were used to characterize his behavior. They told Alex

they would give Clara their full support in putting an end to these behaviors. They said they cared for him and would be willing to help him, but the violence would have to stop.

3. She carried out a sit-down strike for one day, during which family members and friends were invited to visit and help find solutions.

These steps helped Clara regain her self-confidence. She felt she now had the support and staying power to continue with the nonviolent struggle. Alex reacted strongly to the letters and phone calls: he cried when he read the first two letters, and received the other letters and phone calls with restraint and a bowed head. He told people who came to visit on the day of the sit-down strike that his behavior had already changed. His attitude toward his mother and brother became more moderate and warm.

This time the period of calm endured: Alex refrained from violence for a number of weeks and there was not one bad incident until the time of the follow-up. Clara, however, was quite sure Alex would pose her difficult challenges in the future. She viewed the changes in him as perhaps no more than an external adjustment to the new situation. However, she felt the changes she had undergone went deeper: the support she had received and the commitment she had publicly expressed made her feel much more capable to withstand provocations. She knew in her heart that she would not go back to being a passive victim of violence and would no longer put up with Alex's attacks. It had become clear to her that without her tacit consent, the household would not go back to the previous rule of violence.

CASE 3: PRECOCIOUS INDEPENDENCE

Dana was striking in her independence and talent for getting around. Already in the earliest grades, she insisted on buying her school supplies by herself. When the family drove to visit the grandparents, Dana would tell her father how to get there. At age ten she learned to go alone to the post office and the bank. When Marcia and David

(Dana's parents) told a couple of friends that they were sometimes worried about their daughter's independence, the friends humorously replied that they would be glad to borrow Dana for a few weeks, so as to put some order into their lives. Luckily, Dana was a loving daughter and showed no signs of negatively exploiting her independence. All of this changed when she became thirteen.

She got rid of all her old friends and got involved with a group of boys and girls four or five years older than she was. She began coming home late, smoking, and running away from school. She pierced her eyebrow and tongue. She began fighting with her parents and expressing contempt for their conventional ideas and way of life. The parents weren't acquainted with her new friends, except for a sixteen-year-old boy, a self-declared anarchist, with whom she spent days on end. Dana stayed out late almost every night and would sometimes hitchhike home in the early hours. When her mother once tried to stand in her way, when she wanted to go out, Dana shoved her aside and threatened that if she ever tried to stop her again, she would leave the house forever. Sarcastic comments, cursing, and shouting became a routine occurrence; Dana began yelling at her younger sisters as well, and hit them a couple of times.

David and Marcia observed that whenever Dana behaved better toward them, she was about to ask for money. She asked for considerable sums and bought large amounts of clothes (some of which she apparently distributed to her friends). She also demanded services from them with a finality that left no room for objection. For instance, she wavered for a while about joining the school's yearly outing. In the end she decided to go, but phoned home on the first night, saying she was unwell and demanding that her father come to take her home right away. When David asked her to wait until the next day (it was late and the place was four hours' away), she said she would not stay there another night, and he should tell her whether he was coming or not. David bowed to the threat and was glad she was waiting for him when he arrived.

Dana began making sure to be at home mostly at times when her parents were out. Dana's and her parents' lives thus became parallel lines that hardly met. She warned her mother that if she ever appeared at school, she (Dana) would not go back to school again. She warned her parents never to dare contact her friends. The parents felt totally banished from her life.

The parents came to therapy when Dana ran away from home in the wake of a fight with her mother about school. She had phoned home after she had been away for half a day and told Marcia she was in another town, had a job, and was earning a lot of money. Marcia heard laughter in the background. The first therapy session took place on the day after this phone conversation. After the session, the parents reported Dana's disappearance to the police. They then started an extended telephone round. Unfortunately, due to Dana's peremptory threats, they knew only the name and number of Dana's "anarchist" friend. The therapist encouraged them to phone him and also to phone all of her former friends (whose names and telephone numbers they had); perhaps they would know something about Dana's new acquaintances. The friends whom the parents contacted were also asked to call Dana on her cellular phone and establish contact with her. Although there was no answer from the "anarchist" friend's house, one of Dana's former friends told the parents that Dana had been going out with a girl she knew. The parents succeeded in reaching this girl's mother, who told them that her daughter had gone to the Sea of Galilee with two other friends. The parents passed on this information to the police and drove to the area themselves. After a day of searching, they found Dana on a beach, went up to her, and said that they wanted to take her home. They told her that the police was looking for her. Dana noticed their determination and, to their surprise, agreed to go back with them.

Dana locked herself in her room and gave no answer to the parents' questions or entreaties. The parents called the therapist and a session was held over the phone to help them plan their reaction to the event: they decided to hold a sit-down strike of three days. They phoned a large number of friends and relatives, told them what was happening, told them about nonviolent resistance and about the sit-down strike, and asked them to come, sit with them, and help them find a solution. They announced to Dana through the bedroom door that they were taking time off work and that they would all stay home until a solution was found that would allow them to go back to leading a normal life. They inserted a leaflet under her door, enumerating the three life areas that demanded change: Dana's disappearances, cutting school, and physical and verbal violence against them and her sisters. These demands brought Dana out of her room: she came out in a fury, shouting threats. Luckily, the first visitors were already in the house and their presence helped contain Dana's raving. The stream of visits did not abate for the three days of the strike. Marcia's brother and sister alternated sleeping in the house. Dana sometimes closed herself up in her room, sometimes came out and staged verbal attacks (especially between visits), and sometimes engaged in conversation with the visitors. On the first day of the strike, a couple of friends of the family, Eva and George, managed to get closer to Dana. She invited them into her room and held a lengthy conversation, first with the two of them, and then with Eva alone. Eva, especially, began functioning as a mediator between Dana and her parents. The good contact between Dana and Eva persisted also after the strike. The two would meet or hold telephone conversations, sometimes for hours. At the end of such a conversation, Eva would sometimes come out with some compromise suggestion that she had worked up with Dana. These were often far from ideal, but were already a step on the way to some sort of negotiation.

After the sit-down strike, a few days of relative calm ensued. Dana began telling her parents when she was coming back and sticking to some sort of daily schedule. A week later, however, Dana failed to return home at the agreed time. The parents went to look for her at the "anarchist" friend's house and brought her home from there. The next day they performed a sit-in, in the course of which Dana hit her mother. Eva and George were then called in, and Eva closeted herself with Dana for three hours, after which a compromise was reached. From then on the parents always invited friends to be present during the sit-ins: this put an end to the physical violence. Marcia was worried that Eva's closeness to her daughter might stand in the way of an improvement in Dana's direct relationship with her. George agreed with Marcia's view of the matter and convinced Eva to join the parents on a telephone round, when Dana failed to return at the agreed hour once again. This readiness of Eva to take action at the parents' side blurred somewhat the demarcation between the "bad guys" and the "good guys."

It took a while for the parents to become able to withstand provocations and, especially, to refrain from sermonizing. The habit of constant preaching and reprimanding was too ingrained to be stopped overnight. David, especially, described his behavior as a hopeless attempt "to knock sense into Dana's head." Gradually they managed to avoid this trap. In addition, Marcia's creativeness with reconciliation gestures disarmed Dana's oppositional stance. The atmosphere began to thaw.

After four weeks of continuous work of nonviolent resistance interspersed with reconciliation gestures and mediation attempts, Dana's outbursts and late-comings decreased considerably. However, there was no improvement in Dana's attitude to school. The school year finished, and Dana announced that she would not go back to her previous school. She agreed to join her mother on the search for another one. On these occasions the two began to grow closer once again. Dana started giving her mother physical signs of affection, the likes of which Marcia hadn't received for a long time. The search for a new school, however, proved fruitless. Dana found fault with every proposal and seemed bent on stopping school altogether. Recently, she had begun working in a computer service company. Within a few weeks, she had managed to demonstrate her abilities to such an extent that she not only kept her work but also got a raise and improved the marketing strategies of the company. The parents, once again, were able to look at Dana's striking abilities not only with anxiety but also with awe. Dana's amazing success, however, reinforced her in her decision not to go back to school.

At a follow-up session two months later, the parents reported that there had been no more late arrivals or disappearances. To the parents' satisfaction, Dana gave up her relations with her new friends.

The home fights became more "normal" and there were no violent outbursts of any kind. On the other hand, it became more and more clear that a return to school was, for the present, out of the question. When the parents mentioned to Dana that this would constitute an infringement of the law, Dana cut the conversation short by saying: "The law will have to adapt itself to me!"

Expectedly, Marcia and David still had considerable fears for the future. The therapist remarked to them that such fears were not out of place and would help them keep their eyes open. At the end of the follow-up session, Marcia came up with a dream that Dana had related to her. She had dreamed she was in a lonely place at night, when suddenly her grandfather (who had died two years before and to whom Dana had been very close) appeared to her and told her that he was watching her, knew all the things she was doing, and found they were very bad. Dana tried to run away from him, but he kept reappearing and blocking her way. The grandfather said she could not run away from him, for he would be with her wherever she went. After telling her mother this dream, Dana smiled and told her it was good she wasn't meeting with her recent friends anymore. Marcia felt this pronouncement was the greatest gift she had ever received from her daughter. The therapist said this was also one of the most beautiful gifts he had received: a perfect dream about parental presence.

5 VIOLENCE TOWARD SIBLINGS

The harsh facts about the severity and prevalence of parental violence toward children were kept secret for many years. The fog of denial and dismissal was so thick that doctors, therapists, and society at large were reluctant to believe the phenomenon existed, despite recurrent visits to emergency rooms by babies and children suffering wounds and fractures that clearly resembled the results of abuse and despite repeated reports by adults that they had been beaten or abused by their parents as children. The cloak of secrecy was lifted as a result of the efforts of pioneering doctors, feminist organizations, bold therapists, and public figures. Today, Western society is increasingly open to recognizing the horrific facts and prepared to confront the persistent phenomenon of the violence of parents and other adults toward children. Yet on a subject closely related to parental violence, dismissal and denial by the professional community and society at large still reign. The subject is violence toward siblings. According to all research data available, violence toward siblings is much more common than violence by parents toward their children, and no less severe. Finkelhor and Dziuba-Leatherman (1994) found in a comprehensive study that attack by their own siblings is the main cause of physical harm and sexual abuse to children. This study replicated the findings of other studies. Several studies of sexual abuse in the family found that abuse by siblings is more common, endures longer, and is no less traumatic than abuse by parents (Alpert 1991; Boney-McCoy & Finkelhor 1995; DeJong 1989; Finkelhor 1980; Laviola 1992; O'Brien 1991; Smith & Israel 1987).

Findings regarding physical assault are similar: violence toward siblings is more common, more enduring, and no less traumatic than assault by a parent (Loeber, Weissman, & Reid 1983; Steinmetz 1977, 1978; Straus & Gelles 1990). No study to date has contradicted these findings. Nonetheless, societal and professional awareness of the incidence of violence perpetrated by siblings is minimal. Media coverage of violence by siblings is negligible in comparison to the coverage of parental abuse. The attitude of disregard extends to the professional literature as well. Thus, the subject of physical and sexual abuse of children by their parents was addressed in 7,885 articles in the professional literature in the 1990s, while the physical and sexual abuse of children by their siblings was addressed only 37 times.[1] How can this selective blindness be explained?

Two factors militate against awareness. One is the reluctance of parents and children alike to expose the phenomenon. The victim is afraid of exposure, out of fear of the assailant's threats or the parents' reaction. The parents, for their part, try to prevent exposure out of shame and fear of the anticipated consequences for the violent child and the whole family. Reports by parents to the police that one of their children attacked another are very rare, to say nothing of complaints of sexual abuse. Parents almost always prefer to keep the problem secret and deal with it within the household.

The other factor that clouds awareness stems from an ideologically based assumption: the view that children are essentially good and, unless they are grossly warped by their environment, will develop positive relations with their siblings. Violent behavior toward siblings can thus result only from massive neglect and trauma. Thus, if a brother is sexually abusing his sister, he must have been the victim of sexual abuse, in all probability, by his parents. This view automatically transfers the blame to the parents, making the child's violence secondary. The spotlight is thereby aimed at the "real" cause of the problem, namely, adult violence. The unquestionable belief in the child's innocence thus perpetuates the view that the parents are

---

[1] This comparison is based on data from a number of computerized data bases.

the root of all evil and strengthens the selective blindness regarding sibling violence.

The damage of this prevalent view goes beyond the furthering of selective blindness. Therapists who view the parents as automatically suspect avoid giving them effective tools for combating children's violence. The hidden assumption is that strengthening the parents will actually increase their negative power over their children. In this way, therapists may actually be neutralizing the chief factor in the family that could curb sibling violence. In effect, failing to empower the parents may well be tantamount to abandoning the weak siblings to the mercy of the strong and violent one. However, how true is it that a battering or abusive child is actually a battered or abused child?

CAUSES OF VIOLENCE AGAINST SIBLINGS

The prevailing view that a battering or abusive brother is actually a battered or abused child postulates an intergenerational chain of transmission of evil: children who are victims become assailants and will grow up to be battering or abusive husbands or parents in their turn. The parents are thus the original pathogenic factor that defiles the child's innocence and ultimately turns him into a violent adult. Children's violence is nothing but a new manifestation of parental violence. This view draws support from an established research finding: children who were victims of violence or sexual abuse are at a heightened risk of becoming batterers or abusers (de Young 1982; Olweus 1980; Patterson 1982; Smith & Israel 1987).

The nonviolent parent, too, is held suspect in cases of violence between siblings, being guilty of failing to protect the child from his sibling's assault. Adults who were victims of violence or abuse by their siblings in their childhood often have painful memories of their parents' unwillingness to protect them or of the parents' dismissive disregard of all alarm signals. The parent might be blamed, too, when he does intervene, such as when he responds to the battered child's calls for help by hitting the assaulting sibling. This response is of no value to the victim and can actually reinforce the family's violent patterns (Wiehe 1997). Thus the parent is almost always presented in a negative light: he is suspected of being a battering or abusing parent (otherwise his child would not be battering or abusing his sibling); he is guilty of failing to provide adequate protection; and conversely, he is guilty if he does respond to calls for help by attacking the battering child.

Actually, the relation between parental violence and sibling violence is only partial. Indeed, parental violence increases the risk of sibling violence, but is not a necessary or sufficient cause of this violence. Other factors play no less important roles and can lead to violence between siblings even in the complete absence of violence by the parents.

Research among adults who were battered children shows that most of them, far from becoming themselves violent parents or spouses, are actually exceedingly wary of resorting to violence or even to less extreme power-oriented strategies (Gully et al. 1981). Likewise, most victims of sexual abuse are not liable to become abusive adults (this is, after all, obvious: most victims of abuse are women, while most perpetrators are men). It follows that being the victim of violence is not a sufficient condition for becoming violent or abusive. Nor is it a necessary condition. In an in-depth study of family dynamics in twelve cases of sibling sexual abuse, only one of the abusers was found to have been the victim of previous sexual abuse (Adler & Schutz 1995). It seems that in the area of physical violence between siblings, the situation is similar: of the dozens of families in our care where there was violence toward a sibling, only in a few had the assailant been the victim of parental violence. Other variables, then, are needed to explain the development of children's violence.

LACK OF PARENTAL PRESENCE

The factor found to be decisive in most studies of children's violence in general, and of violence toward siblings in particular, is the lack of parental presence. The less able the parents are to establish their presence in the household, the higher the risk of the child's being violent. A study conducted at Tel Aviv University found that when parents felt helpless and lacked presence, the risk of sibling violence rose. This finding emerged independently in the testimonies of the parents and those of the battered children (Burla-Galili 2001). The lack of parental presence can be physical, systemic, or emotional.

1. *Lack of physical presence.* Children who live in single-parent households are at a particularly high risk of developing violent and antisocial behavior patterns (Loeber & Hay 1997). A study of 7,000 boys and their families showed that boys who grew up in single-parent families are more frequently involved in violent and criminal activities (Dornbusch et al. 1985). The risk of such a pattern developing drops when another adult lives in the household in addition to the single parent. This adult makes up, to some extent, for the absence of the other parent. Steinberg (1987) checked the degree to which children who grew up with one or two parents were susceptible to a criminal suggestion by an older peer (who was a confederate of the researcher). Children who grew up with one parent were found to be much more susceptible. These data suggest that the absence of one parent creates a deficiency in presence, which the remaining parent is hard pressed to fill. In such cases, chances are also high that the aggressive child will fill the parental vacuum by overpowering his siblings.

Other forms of parental physical unavailability have a similar effect. Thus in homes where the parents work for long hours, the children display higher levels of violence (Funk 1996). Parental unavailability due to physical or mental illness was also found to be related to high levels of children's violence in general, and against siblings in particular (Downey & Coyne 1990; Ratzke & Cierpka 1999; Schweitzer 1987, 1997).

2. *Lack of systemic presence.* "Systemic presence" is when parents and children have the experience that the environment supports the parents and provides them with social confirmation (Omer 2000). Parents do not operate in a vacuum but are subject to the influence of their spouses and the people, institutions, and community among

whom they live. Parents who do not have the support of a partner, relatives, or friends are in a position of systemic weakness in relation to the aggressive child (Wahler 1980). Parental weakness is directly related to the absence of social support. Research shows, for instance, that when the father leaves the household (in the case of divorce), the level of violent behavior of children toward the mother and the other siblings rises (Hetherington et al. 1975). This rise in aggressiveness is usually interpreted as a sign of emotional distress, but there is another possible explanation: the mother was weakened by the father's departure. The same researchers found, for instance, that when the mother receives greater support from the community, the levels of violence are considerably lower.

Another source of systemic weakness is secrecy. Many parents choose to keep the violent child's actions secret to protect the child's or the family's good name. This reduces systemic presence by isolating the parents and blocking potential help. In such cases, siblings often pay the price for the desire to keep family events secret.

Systemic weakness can also be the result of a marginal or negatively involved father. Patterson (1980) showed that the more positively involved the father is in the child's upbringing, the less the chances of the child being violent.

Prolonged conflict between the parents is also a breeding ground for child violence in general, and violence against siblings in particular (Dadds & Powell 1991; Jouriles et al. 1991). In effect, when the parents undermine each other, the aggressive child's freedom of action expands, with predictable negative effects.

Also, professional figures may inadvertently undermine parental presence. Therapists often maintain that siblings should be left alone to resolve their conflicts. This position, which may be appropriate for routine squabbles, becomes dangerous where the potential for violence or abuse is higher. In these cases, the professional advice may lower the parents' vigilance to negative developments. The "quiet" that is supposedly achieved is sometimes the result of the weak child's realizing that the parents won't help, and that therefore there is no choice but to give in to the strong sibling's demands.

The data about lack of systemic presence abet the similar ones about the lack of physical presence. In both cases, the potentially violent child fills the vacuum left by the parents and establishes himself in a position of power.

3. *Lack of parental presence for emotional or ideological reasons.* As stated earlier, permissive ideologies may further behavioral problems of all kinds. The effect of a permissive ideology on sibling violence is obvious: the permissive parent prefers not to intervene. In effect, the permissive ideology glorifies the parent's abdication of any limit-setting role. One of the negative results of this stance is that the weak child may be wholly left to the mercy of the violent one.

Parental presence is also weakened by feelings of guilt, pity, and anxiety. Guilt, pity, and anxiety are interrelated: guilt feeds pity, and the two ensure a steady supply of anxiety. When these feelings dominate, the parental voice may become a whimper. The parents may then lean more and more toward surrender, which in turn leads to an increase in the child's violence (Patterson 1982; Patterson et al. 1992).

THE BIOLOGICAL FACTOR
(THE CHILD WITH SPECIAL NEEDS)

In therapeutic and educational discourse about children with behavior problems, raising the issue of innate tendencies is considered "politically incorrect," and this for obvious reasons: the label "biological" or "hereditary" supposedly absolves the environment from the responsibility to treat the problem, except for medical treatments. Saying there are innate tendencies would then be tantamount to the declaration: "It's genetic! There's nothing to do about it!" To refute such a conclusion it suffices to look at the way society treats other biologically based problems. A child with learning disabilities, for instance, receives remedial teaching; a child with poor muscle tone receives physiotherapy; and a child with speech difficulties receives speech therapy. Likewise, children with the innate risk of developing violent behaviors deserve special treatment to address their unique needs and risks. These children actually need a greater investment by their parents and their environment. Ignoring the innate aspects of the tendency toward violence and placing the full responsibility on the parents only reduces the possibility of helping the parents expend efforts in the desired direction. Paradoxically, avoiding discussing the biological basis of violent tendencies leads to an attitude of blaming the parents that more than anything harms the therapeutic alliance with them and drastically diminishes the possibilities of preventive or remedial action.

The professional community's avoidance of mentioning innate tendencies cannot change the clear feeling that many parents of aggressive children have, that is, that these children are actually different from the start. Parents often describe these children as impulsive, risk-prone, or as lacking in concentration or inhibition already from the earliest age. Developmental research upholds these impressions: some children do display such tendencies from earliest infancy, and these children are at a high risk of developing violent patterns.

The central concept in the study of innate tendencies is "temperament" (Rothbart & Bates 1998). Temperament is the basic assortment of features that describe the individual's characteristic modes of response. Temperament is not the same as personality but is one of the main factors in determining it. Personality is the fabric that develops as the result of the meeting of temperament and environment. Therefore, the same temperament can lead to very different kinds of personality, depending on the environment in which the child grows up. The best-known characterization of the different features of temperament is that of Thomas and Chess (1977). Among these features are level of activity (e.g., hyperactive children have particularly high levels of activity), reaction threshold (some children will react to even very weak stimuli), intensity of reaction (some children will have a strong reaction even to medium- or low-intensity stimuli), attention span (children with low attention spans often develop learning problems), and emotional tone (some children have a tendency toward irritability, others toward anxiety). These temperamental tendencies have proved stable throughout life (Rothbart &

Bates 1998). Thus, babies characterized shortly after birth as irritable tended to remain that way for the rest of their development (Rothbart Posner, & Rosicky 1994).

One important temperament parameter that is linked to the development of violent behavior is a strong attraction to pleasurable stimuli and a relatively low level of aversion to pain. Indeed, certain children have a strong need for immediate satisfaction and are relatively undeterred by pain or punishment. The parents of such children may find their response to disciplinary measures is not comparable to their attraction to pleasure (Patterson 1980). In addition, because of their relatively low aversion to pain, these children may be more prone to engage in risky behavior (Matheny 1991). The conclusion regarding such children is not "it's genetic, so there is nothing to do about it," but quite the opposite: these children require a particularly high parental investment and a greater amount of consistent supervision and discipline in order to develop the necessary restraints.

Children who go on to develop violent patterns often have temperament features such as a high reaction intensity and a lower reaction to pain or other punishments. Many of these children are also hyperactive and have a short attention span (Bates et al. 1998; Moffit 1990; Moffit & Henry 1991). These children are at high risk and therefore have special needs. They surely need love and acceptance no less than any other children, but parental giving in these areas cannot make up for their unique deficiency. This calls rather for a higher degree of parental supervision and for clear, steady, and effective limits. When these are supplied, these children can gradually strengthen those areas in which they suffer from an inborn weakness. This claim is broadly supported by developmental studies: the violence level of these children is lower, the more clear and consistent the parental ability to supervise them and set them limits (Bates et al. 1998; Florsheim et al. 1998; Hetherington et al. 1975).

Experience shows that acknowledging the temperamental factor, while helping the parents to restore their parental presence, far from discouraging the parents, actually increases their motivation. These parents often feel that for the first time, the therapist understands them, instead of blaming them for the situation. The use of terms such as "biological factors" or "genetic tendencies" does not weaken their determination or lead them to shirk their responsibility. On the contrary, parents often nod their heads in agreement on hearing the truth they have always known, becoming thereby more ready to fulfill their children's special needs.

Research in behavioral genetics has done much to shed light on the relationship that may evolve between parents and children with these special needs. Thus, adopted children who had violent biological mothers tend to arouse more angry responses in their adoptive parents than do adopted children whose biological mothers were not violent (the adoptive parents knew nothing about the biological mothers' violent tendencies). Unfortunately, the adoptive parents' angry and frustrated responses actually strengthen their children's violent patterns. Thus a vicious circle is set up, reinforcing the child's problematic tendencies (Ge et al. 1996; Neiderhiser et al. 1999; O'Connor et al. 1998; Plomin, Chipuer, & Loehlin 1990a; Plomin, Nitz, & Rowe 1990b). Parental understanding of this vicious circle may help mobilize them into a program of nonviolent resistance.

It is, of course, vital to understand that the child's temperament does not work in a vacuum and that parental reactions influence the child's tendencies. This has been clearly demonstrated in a series of studies on biological children of violent parents who were adopted at a young age. Thus, adopted children of violent biological mothers who were raised by parents who were also violent were at a four times higher risk of developing violent patterns than children who were raised by nonviolent adoptive parents (Bohman 1996; Cadoret et al. 1983; Moffit 1990). These findings bring us back to the influence of parental violence on the growing child.

PARENTAL VIOLENCE

We have seen that the prevailing view that child violence is necessarily the outcome of parental violence does not square with research findings. Parental violence is neither a sufficient nor a necessary condition for child violence. But it is a substantial risk factor for aggravating problematic temperamental tendencies. Its effect in this direction works in various ways.

Violent parents usually exhibit deficient parental presence. Violent fathers, for instance, often have little involvement in the child's life, while violent mothers are often helpless. These ineffectual parents may be tempted to restore their control by violent means. This pattern was described as "hit and run parenting" (Omer 2000). Such pronounced swings between helplessness and sharp outbursts are indeed typical of many parents of violent children (Bugental et al. 1989, 1993, 1997; Patterson 1980, 1982; Patterson & Capaldi 1991). This situation contributes variously to the escalation of violence: (1) the lack of parental presence creates an authority vacuum, which the child with difficult temperamental features may try to fill by using violent behavior; (2) the parents' sporadic outbursts contribute to the escalation by raising the level of violence in the family; and (3) the violent parent provides the child with a role model that legitimates violent behavior. The parent's own violence thus points to a path that the child may take if he only dares.

VICTIM AVAILABILITY

For many people, violence becomes a way of life. It grows into a key tool in their daily lives, familial relations, and livelihoods. Children who were the victims of parental violence are indeed at a higher risk of becoming violent adults, but there is a missing link in this description: that the child destined to develop a career of violence also needs to "practice" being an aggressor. This "practice ground" is provided chiefly by the family. Thus it is the child whose family has provided him with available and handy victims who will, in all probability, develop a violent lifestyle. Without such victims at home, this child will have a harder time "advancing" his violent career. This conclusion somewhat overturns the prevailing assumption of popular psychology. It turns out that the battering adult was not necessarily a battered child, but was almost invariably a battering child. Research consistently shows that the best predictor of violence in adulthood is the practice of violence against siblings (or parents), rather than being a recipient of such violence (Gully 1981). In a pioneering study of teenagers arrested for assault outside the home, it was found that the arrest was preceded by a long history of severe violence against siblings and parents (mainly mothers; Loeber et al. 1983). The researchers hypothesized that the family had served these youngsters as a convenient and safe "training ground." Two studies have also reported that violent boys more frequently have older sisters than older brothers (Farrington & West 1971; Loeber et al. 1983). The researchers assumed that older brothers may be less convenient targets of violence than older sisters. Findings such as these are changing the position of professionals toward sibling fighting. Whereas once they advocated nonintervention by parents, the emerging view today is that nonintervention may, in many cases, encourage the aggressor, while leaving the victim helpless and unprotected (Bennett 1990; Perlman & Ross 1997).

"In-house training," however, is not a sufficient condition for creating a broad career of violence. To expand his violent style to situations outside the home, the violent child must develop additional skills. These are "optimally" acquired in a crime-saturated social environment or by joining a gang of delinquents (Henggeler 1991; Moffit 1993).

It seems, then, that a criminal career, like any other career, requires lengthy training and that the opportunity to "practice" plays a central role in this training. That is why it is so important to curb the child's progress along this path. Such a parental attempt may have a highly positive effect, even if the parents are successful only partially and only for a few years. For during the time the child's aggressive behavior is blocked, his criminal training is interrupted, and he may "lag behind" in the development of these negative skills. During this time he may also learn to evolve some nonviolent solutions to his problems. This process decreases the chances that he will choose a criminal career in the future.

To sum up: children with the highest risk of becoming violent have temperaments characterized by restlessness, a low stimulus threshold, strong reactivity, strong attraction to pleasure, and low aversion to pain and punishment. Such children are "all over the place." When such a child grows up without a clear parental presence, his restless and expansive behavior patterns may become sharper and more clearly violent. If the parents are themselves violent, the situation worsens because of the escalation and legitimization of the violent behavior. The availability of unprotected victims in the family further consolidates the child's violence. Nonviolent resistance may be a particularly effective way of countering these negative processes, for it increases parental presence, protects the victims, reduces escalation, and delegitimizes violence.

Counseling programs for the parents of violent children are effective to the extent they help the parents increase their presence and block the violence without escalation. This goal is not identical to strengthening the family hierarchy while placing the parents at its top. Such a focused hierarchical goal fails to take the danger of escalation into account. In effect, a determined effort to strengthen the family hierarchy may turn the home into a battlefield, where parents and children vie for supremacy.

The danger of escalation is also the weak point of many programs based on reward and punishment. Using punishments as a central tool may lead to escalation, especially among aggressive adolescents. These children, as we know, do not accept punishments passively but are likely to respond in kind. This explains the decreasing willingness of parents of violent children to apply behavioral programs the older the child gets (Dishion & Patterson 1992). These parents are afraid of the child's retaliation and therefore are loath to stick to a program that requires punishment as a main tenet.

Likewise, consultation programs that are wholly based on acceptance, warmth, and dialogue with the child may have little relevance to the parents of a violent child, because these programs do not give the parents effective tools to curb the violence or effectively protect the family. If we consider the plight of the violent child's siblings, we may well conclude that programs based on unconditional empathy toward the aggressor miss their humane goal by perpetuating the victims' suffering.

KINDS OF VIOLENCE AGAINST SIBLINGS

Violence against siblings can be grossly divided into physical violence, emotional abuse, and sexual abuse. Physical violence almost always goes with emotional abuse, and sexual abuse with physical violence.

Physical Violence

One of the most prominent researchers into domestic violence asserts that violence among siblings is the most entrenched and common form of violence in society (Finkelhor 1995). Yet it is the least reported kind, and the one that draws the least public interest.

To assess the dimensions of the problem, we must set aside the reports of parents (who usually minimize the phenomenon) and listen to the battered children's own reports. Such an analysis reveals that some 90 percent of all cases of domestic violence fall into this category (Kolko, Kazdin, & Day 1996). The high frequency and the normative acceptance of the phenomenon ("That's the way it is between siblings!") bewilder the parents: should they intervene, when, and how?

The question of parental intervention is a function of the following questions.

Is there a substantial difference between the siblings in age or power?

Are there signs that the violence is being applied in an effort to control the sibling, such as forcing his obedience or dictating his behavior?

Are there signs of humiliation?

Does the violence typically escalate? Is it getting worse with time?

Does the violence lead to a clear division of roles: strong-weak, commander-obeyer?

The more salient these characteristics, the more called for is parental intervention.

Physical violence toward siblings has many forms. The most common are pushing, slapping, punching, kicking, biting, scratching, and hair pulling. The use of implements such as sticks, rubber hoses, belts, hairbrushes, knives, and scissors is not uncommon. Particularly frightening forms of this violence may be choking (with bare hands or with pillows), holding over high drops, or dunking in water. One of the less common but quite painful forms of physical violence is tickling (against the tickled sibling's will). Sometimes tickling persists to the point of crying, vomiting, or loss of consciousness. Physical violence is often a collective act, with a group of siblings beating another sibling in a sort of repetitive torture ritual.

Emotional Abuse

The impact of emotional abuse is no less severe, and it is more elusive and harder to identify than physical violence (Wolfe 1987). Familiarity with some typical manifestations of this kind of violence may help identify it. The most common forms are: derisive name-calling ("fatso," "cow," "pig," "moron," "retard," "farter," and "tattletale"), mockery, and deliberate denigration of the victim. The abusive brother often invites other children to join the festival of insults. Often added to the derogatory names are insulting rhymes and tunes, which the abusive brother sings in public. Other common modes of torture are mocking mimicry of some of the victim's traits or physical attributes (stutter, asthmatic whistle, way of chewing, learning disability, motor disability), pestering about certain of the victim's activities, or publicizing intimate information about the victim (the onset of her menstrual period, bra-wearing, or bed-wetting).

Deliberate statements aimed at denigrating the victim, often told repeatedly as stories, can be very damaging to the sibling, such as her having been an unwanted child, her having been born due to an "accident," how the parents wanted to get rid of her and that actually she belongs in the garbage, or that the sibling is not the parents' biological child, that she was switched in the hospital, or that she is actually an adopted child, as evident by the color of her skin. These messages contain the overt or covert conclusion that "it would have been better if you didn't exist." Such messages can be disastrous if they become part of the victim's self-image.

Another means of injuring self-esteem is systematic ignoring. Parents have a particularly hard time confronting this strategy, because the attacking sibling is "actually not doing anything." The victim's degradation may also be achieved by imposing chores to show who is the boss, such as forcing the victim to clean up after the assailant. The theme of control is central to many cases of abuse.

Another cruel form of pestering is the sadistic exploitation of the victim's fears. Thus, the siblings of children afraid of the dark, of animals, or of getting lost may expose their siblings to these situations for their own pleasure or for the purpose of blackmail. The assaulting sibling sometimes stages quite elaborate situations to achieve the desired effect. For instance, a woman who was the victim of abuse by a sister seven years her senior reports: "She would go to the phone and pretend she was calling a man called Mr. Crunch, who ran a place for 'bad children.' She would make an appointment for him to come take me forever" (Wiehe 1997: 51). Among the families in our project we encountered the following case: a girl who had suffered from bed-wetting until the age of twelve was astonished to discover at fifteen that the problem had recurred. This led to a deterioration of her mood and to severe social avoidance. About two months after the bed-wetting returned, the parents found out that her older brother, eighteen, was waking up in the middle of the night, sneaking into her room, and urinating in his sister's bed.

The victim sibling's cherished possessions may also become targets of the abusive sibling's schemes. A favorite doll, for instance, can become the object of a cruel ritual with the abusive sibling poking out its eye, cutting off its ear, and chopping off its head (Wiehe 1997). A particularly extreme variation on this theme is the torture or slaughter of a pet belonging to the victim.

Sexual Abuse

Many people tend to minimize the significance of sexual games between siblings. There is a tendency to view such games as a natural part of growth and development. This view may perhaps be appropriate when the contact is an expression of curiosity about bodily differences and when the age difference between the siblings is small. How can parents know whether this interest has crossed the line or is approaching actual abuse? The following features can help them make this judgment:

The age difference between the siblings is at least three years.

There are signs of the use of threats or force.

The "games" include oral sex, penetration, or contacts aimed at achieving orgasm.

The "games" include additional participants (siblings or friends of the assailing sibling).

Even when the "sex games" are between siblings close in age, the younger sibling's consent may not be real. The phrase "pseudo-consent" was coined in the literature regarding sexual abuse among siblings to describe relations between siblings close in age where it is doubtful whether the actions are undertaken out of free volition or under duress or deceit (Bank & Kahn 1982; Laviola 1992).

In many cases of sexual abuse between siblings, the parents are not aware of what is happening. This is different from sexual abuse by a parent, where usually even the parent who is not actively involved in the abuse knows to some extent what is going on. The authors of the most comprehensive book on this topic (Caffaro & Conn-Caffaro 1998) say that even when parents are very alert, sexual abuse between siblings may remain hidden from view. But the danger of prolonged concealment is significantly diminished, the greater the parental presence.

DETECTING VIOLENCE AGAINST SIBLINGS

Violence against siblings is more elusive, less reported, and taken less seriously than parental violence. Parents and professionals should therefore pay special attention to a number of sources that can reveal the hidden information. The first and most important source is the victim's signs of distress, whether they appear at home or at school. Today professionals are very aware of the fact that a child showing signs of depression, anxiety, isolation, self-injury, or eccentric behavior may be a victim of domestic violence. But professional attention focuses almost exclusively on possible abuse by parents, whereas the possibility of the more common abuse, by siblings, is often overlooked and is not seriously explored.

A child's signs of distress should serve as warnings to the parents, too. A child who avoids the company of his sibling, cries when left alone with her, seeks the parent's company more than before, or shows unusual signs of fear (relative to himself), sadness, isolation, or sleep disturbances is sending signals requiring inquiry. Parental observation of interactions between the siblings or direct questioning of the child (in an atmosphere of parental support) may lead to disclosure. Another indication of potential violence toward siblings is the violent behavior of one of the siblings outside the home. As we have seen, a child who is violent outside the home is likely to be violent also within the home. A child who hits, humiliates, or exploits other children is very likely to do the same to her siblings if only given the chance to do so. Exploring the situation at home in such cases may reveal violence toward siblings. Another warning sign is the existence of violence toward the parents. In our work with parents who were the victims of violence by their children, we often found the child was also violent toward his siblings.

Caffaro and Conn-Caffaro (1998) developed guidelines for an interview to detect violence toward siblings. The guidelines enable parents to perform an initial assessment by themselves. They can even try answering some of the questions without asking the children directly, by referring to their own observations. In areas where they feel they do not know enough, they should direct the questions to the presumed victims. This questioning has a double objective: to obtain the information and to display parental supervision and presence.[2]

QUESTIONS ABOUT INTIMIDATION, COERCION, AND SILENCING

What would your brother do if you told your parents something he didn't want you to tell?

When your brother is mad at you, what are you most afraid will happen?

When your sister annoys you or picks on you, does she stop if you ask her to?

Does your sister try to scare you sometimes?

Does your brother touch you sometimes in ways you don't like?

What do you do when your brother wants you to do something you don't want to do?

Does your brother ask you to keep things that you know are wrong secret?

Give me an example of something your sister did to you that she would not do in front of me.

QUESTIONS ABOUT GUILT FEELINGS AND FEELINGS OF UNPROTECTEDNESS

If your sister hits you, whose fault is it?

If your brother touches you in a way you think is wrong, whose fault is it?

[2] The following questions are selected and adapted from Caffaro & Conn-Caffaro (1998).

If your brother hit you, would you tell your parents? Would they help you?

If your brother touched you in a way you think is wrong, would you tell your parents? Would they help you?

QUESTIONS ABOUT HUMILIATION

Does your brother shout at you a lot? Insult you? Criticize you? Call you names?

Does your sister embarrass you or humiliate you in front of others?

Do you sometimes think something is wrong with you because of something your brother did to you or said to you?

QUESTIONS ON THE EXPERIENCE OF PARENTAL PRESENCE

How much time do you and your sister spend at home alone?[3]

In every family there are things the parents notice more and things they notice less. What are the things in your house your parents notice most? What do they notice less? Are there things you wish your parents would notice more?

What does your mother do when she sees you and your brother fighting? What does your father do?

QUESTIONS TO THE PARENTS

If your daughter complains that her brother hits her, do you believe her? Why not?

If your daughter complains her sister humiliates or abuses her, do you believe her? Why not?

---

[3] The following questions are intended for interviews conducted by professionals.

Did your daughter ever complain her brother touched her sexually? Did you believe her? Why not?

Sometimes siblings "pick" on each other. Tell me what it is like between your children, and what you do.

Sometimes siblings try to embarrass each other with words or actions related to the body or sexuality. Does that happen among your children? What do you do?

Where do you draw the line for your children as far as their sexual behavior or curiosity?

Tell me a little about how your children fight with each other. How do you react?

Are you ever concerned that one sibling might hurt another?

In many cases, violence between siblings occurs not unilaterally but in the form of scuffles between two children of relatively equal ability. Such violence, too, can be dangerous and cause physical and emotional harm. The principles and methods of nonviolent resistance are relevant for dealing with this kind of violence as well.

FIGHTING SIBLING VIOLENCE BY NONVIOLENT RESISTANCE

We have seen that the prevailing assumption that parental abuse is the real cause of violence toward siblings is little more than a widespread dogma. This blaming stance toward parents precludes any possibility of building a therapeutic alliance with them. Professionals thus jettison in advance their main potential collaborators in the fight against the child's violence. In effect, we can hope to cope with the hidden endemic problem of violence toward siblings only by moving beyond the prevailing accusatory stance and evolving an attitude of trust toward parents who are willing to get help. We therapists should approach these parents with the assumption that they are motivated by true concern and an honest desire to help their children and themselves. Viewing the parents as defensive, as sabotaging the therapy, as trying to invade their child's privacy, or as bent on preventing her independence are professional habits generated by the erroneous view of the parents as the main pathogenic factor. What the therapist views as a parent's resistance to treatment is often nothing but a reflection of the parent's feeling that the therapist's suggestions are not helping. Parents respond very differently when offered an acceptable and practicable program such as nonviolence resistance. Far from reacting defensively, they then display an impressive willingness to get to work. And yet a number of factors may stand in the way of a clearly trusting stance by professionals.

1. When the parents respond to the violence between siblings by ignoring it or with their own violence.

2. When parents express negative and critical feelings toward the violent child, thereby giving the impression they are rejecting parents.

3. When the professional fears that a display of trust on his part will reduce his vigilance and undermine his ability to uncover incidents of abuse and violence by the parents.

We think these considerations do not invalidate the urgent need for a more trusting attitude that would enable the establishment of a good working alliance with parents. In effect, the therapists' understandable concerns could have a far better repercussion on the family, if the therapist kept the following in mind.

1. The fact that many parents ignore violence toward siblings or respond to it with violence shows that these parents feel powerless and that they are caught in escalation processes. This in itself does not disqualify them as working partners. Parents realize they are helpless and that the situation is worsening, and this leads them to welcome any real alternative that can liberate them from the trap. Nonviolent resistance provides just the alternative they seek, by freeing them both from their helplessness and from the escalation.

2. Parents of violent children develop strong feelings of frustration and anger. Often such parents express their wish to banish the child from the home. Such statements give the professional the impression that parental rejection lies at the root of the problem. This view often leads the parent to entrench herself in a defensive position. Nonviolent resistance, in contrast, enables us to view the parent's feelings as resulting from helplessness and from escalation processes. The adoption of a stance of nonviolent resistance by the parents may therefore help to dissolve the anger and lead to the reemergence of positive feelings. Many parents respond to this description of their plight and of the options available to them with enthusiasm. They reminisce about their positive feelings toward their child with longing and express deep pain over the near disappearance of those feelings from their lives. The hope that nonviolent resistance may lead to a return of these positive feelings makes them embrace the strategy full-heartedly.

3. We must remember that abusive parents do not come to therapy unless they were forced to do so by the authorities following the discovery of their maltreatment. Otherwise, these parents are chiefly interested in keeping their secret, and nothing endangers that more than seeking therapy. One may then conclude that most of the parents who come to therapy without being forced to do so by a court of law are not in the category of abusive parents. Their violence, if there is any, is mostly episodic and reactive. Such episodes are less damaging than the violence of abusive parents. Among the hundreds of parents we treated there were several cases where the parents had violent outbursts toward their children (before the therapy). But there was not one case among them where the child required medical treatment following the parents' outbursts. However, we did encounter several cases where the parents or siblings of the violent child required medical treatment or even hospitalization before the parents came to therapy. The transition to a parental strategy of nonviolent resistance led then to a sharp drop in the level of violence both by the aggressive child and by the parents. Therefore, renunciation of

the therapist's vigilant, suspicious attitude in favor of trusting the parents paid off.

PRACTICAL STEPS

1. *Openly addressing domestic violence.* The principle of openness is paramount in treating violence toward siblings. This violence thrives in the dark. An open or even public parental attitude may in its own right change the violence's survival conditions to the point of making it impossible. Inside the family, explicit words should be employed, such as "violence toward your brother" or "emotional abuse." All members of the family (except for very little children) should be informed about the fight against the violence. The parents must declare that they will demand ongoing reports and will check themselves whether the violence really ceased. The victim must be encouraged to tell the parents about any violent episodes.

Speaking openly with all the members of the family makes it possible to recruit them and expands the circle of people who will help act against the violence. The siblings should be told the whole family is now engaged in a fight against the violence. The violent child can take part in the fight by acting against his own violence and by joining the fight against other displays of violence that may occur in the home. This way, a distinction is made between the violent behavior and the violent child. The fight is against the behavior, not against the child.

The parents should address members of the family thus: "We – Dad, Mom and all of you together (they should each be named, including the violent child) – will no longer succumb to violence, will no longer let it take place out of view, will no longer cooperate with it and will not remain silent when we see it! Every time you see an episode of hitting, humiliating, name-calling, intimidation, or threats, you must tell us. We will not punish but we will act resolutely to stop the violence. We will also protect the child who tells us, and not let anything bad happen to him. In addition, here are the telephone numbers of other people who have agreed to help us. If necessary, when we are not home, or if you prefer to tell somebody else, you can call them. It is not being a tattletale!" In this way, all of the siblings can become part of the "we" who are fighting the violence.

If the parents have doubts as to the truth of the reports (such doubts are natural and sometimes justified), they must strengthen their acts of supervision and guarding, without taking an accusatory line toward the assaulting child or a minimizing tone toward the complaining child. A parental response to the denials of a child accused of assault can be, for instance: "True or not, we are going to tighten our supervision and guarding, to further reduce the chances of such a thing happening!" Such a statement strengthens the victim's confidence without encouraging "false accusations." False accusations do exist, but suspicions of them must not lead to dismissal. An explicit statement by the parents that they are increasing their supervision (backed, of course, by actions) will reduce the chances of violence without rewarding false accusations. The parents' objective is to achieve security, not to "decide who is right."

2. *Encouraging the victim.* The parents must encourage the victim to relate the full and detailed story of the violence. They must help the victim tell and even document (in writing or with a tape recorder) the events, preferably in front of witnesses in whose presence the victim feels safe.

Besides recruiting the witnesses as supporters of the nonviolent resistance campaign, the documentation also has a therapeutic dimension. Bringing the facts to light in front of witnesses who support the victim's right to speak and receive protection strengthens him. The witnesses who hear the story must express their willingness to act in defense of the victim. The assailant must know the testimony is being taken, and must be allowed to look at it if she wants to. If the assailant denies some of the testimony, neither the denial nor the testimony should be rejected. In case of doubt, it should be stated: "We cannot determine whether all the details are true. Therefore we are going to increase our supervision and guarding, so that things like this can not happen in the future!" To the child's protests (whether the assailant or the victim) over the parents' lack of trust, the parents may respond: "Our trust is limited. Our supervision and guarding will fill the void where our trust cannot be complete!" The attitude of "limited trust" allows the parents to take both sides' claims seriously, without accusing either of them of lying. In the literature about violence toward siblings (e.g., Wiehe 1997), there is a demand that the parents always believe the victim's complaints. This demand is understandable considering the desire to protect the victim and prevent further trauma by expressing disbelief. But this demand is impossible to fulfill for many parents, especially if the complaining child has been caught lying before. The attitude proposed here allows protection of the victim and encouragement of reporting, without the parents being required to squelch their doubts. For the victim, the turning point is the parents' transition to nonviolent resistance, that is, to an attitude of increased supervision and protection. These goals can be achieved even from a stance of "limited trust."

3. *Exposing the secret and including outside helpers.* Exposing the secret within the family does not have the same impact as revealing it beyond the family. In a sense, the violent child takes his family for granted, especially when the parents are viewed as weak or helpless. Including additional people (friends, relatives, and community figures, such as a social worker, a school guidance counselor, or a clergyman) is a powerful tool. Naturally, the decision to bring outside helpers into the secret can be very difficult. But even in cases where disclosure is hardest, the parents should make the effort to find at least one person outside the family (besides the therapist) to act as witness and tell the assailant and the victim that he knows the facts and is working with the parents to stop the violence. Crossing the family line is critical to the transition to nonviolent resistance.

One of the chief goals of exposing the secret is to extricate the parents and the victim from their loneliness. We advise parents to turn to a number of people and tell them about the violent episodes and about the nonviolent resistance program. It is advisable to give each one of them a copy of the instructions to parents. Familiarity with the program leads to an improvement in people's willingness to cooperate and helps to remove doubts that often stem from the dominant parent-blaming assumptions.

The parents should ask each of their supporters to address the violent child by person, phone, letter, fax, or e-mail and tell him that they heard a detailed description of the violent episodes. The multitude of messages through a variety of means increases the message's impact. When addressing the child, these people must stress that such behavior is called "domestic violence" (or "sibling abuse" or "sexual abuse"), and that it is not only intolerable, but also a serious breach of the law. Therefore, they are committed to helping the parents act with determination to stop the violence. The supporters must add that they care about him (the assailant) and that they want to maintain a good and positive relationship with him, but the violence has to stop completely. The supporters must also address the victim and tell him that they know about the violence and are committed to helping the parents put an end to it.

The victim must know that he is no longer alone and that if he feels the need, he can call and ask for their help. The supporters should give the victim their phone numbers and make sure he took them down correctly. Likewise, they must make further contact (in person and by phone) with the assailant, the victim, and the parents.

Including a public officer (such as a social worker or a probation officer) can make an important contribution to reducing the violence. Parents fear that involving such figures may lead to the violent child's removal from the home or open a criminal record against him, harming his future. This is much less likely to happen if the parents go to these authorities with the therapist and present a detailed plan of nonviolent resistance. Officials who witness the family and the therapeutic system mobilizing to deal with the problem are likely to back the parents' efforts.

Deciding to bring in the police is always hard for the parents, but it is better to do so as part of the therapeutic program with the participation of the therapist (who may have an influence on the way the case is treated, and even on its future closure), rather than as a last resort, when the damage is greater and the options much more limited.

Exposing the secret and including outside people often lead to strong emotional responses in the aggressor. He may accuse his parents of betrayal, sever ties with them, lock himself in his room, spread negative stories about them, or run away from home. Therefore, at this time, the parents should increase their guarding not only of the victim but also of the assailant. They must prepare for the possibility of an escape and ready themselves for an extended telephone round or tailing endeavor.

The help of friends and relatives may be decisive in dealing with this crisis. Therapists must help the parents understand that nondisclosure of the secret amounts to a perpetuation of the violence. In the many dozens of cases we treated or supervised, where parents acted according to instructions to break the cover of secrecy, there was a rapid and sharp drop in the violence. Only in one case did the assailant run away from home for a few days (the parents managed to maintain contact with him throughout the days of his escape). In two cases, children declared a boycott of silence against their parents. In these cases, too, the violent children maintained ongoing contact with at least one of the outside helpers, which allowed for mediation and a gradual cancellation of the boycott. In no case did the boycott last more than one month, and in no case did the child respond with a mental breakdown or a suicide attempt.

4. *Presence and supervision.* Beyond the initial acts of disclosure and recruitment of help, the parents must take actions that display parental presence and supervision. At the beginning, the periods of time the assailant spends with the victim unsupervised must be minimized. The supervision process is time consuming, but it would be a mistake to presume the violence could be curbed without this investment. The parents must display their presence by personal chaperoning, frequent phone contact, daily debriefing, increased presence of other relatives (grandparents, for instance, can be very helpful, if they are carefully instructed as to the importance of full reports to the parents of every incident of violence), frequent phone calls by the

external supporters, and equipping the victim with the phone numbers of the supporters she can call if necessary. All the presence and
supervision measures must be described clearly to both the assailant
and the victim.

5. *Nonviolence resistance measures as a response to continued instances
of violence.* The measures described above make it much harder to
continue the violence. Still, the violent child will sometimes try to
bully her victim again, while declaring overtly or covertly: "Let's just
see what they do to me!" The parents should then stick to the program of nonviolent resistance, taking steps such as delaying their
reaction (but immediately separating the assailant from the victim),
avoiding escalation, conducting sit-ins, and transmitting messages
from external parties.

The parents should document the new violent episodes in detail,
to enable the mobilization of "public opinion." The written documentation should be passed on to the assailant with a list of names,
including people connected with the family and people she cares
about, such as her friends and their parents, her sports coach, and
people at school. She should be told that if the violence recurs, the
document, with the detailed description of the additional violent
acts, will be sent to all the people on the list. The parents must add:
"We are not prepared to tolerate any other violence and we decided
not to stay alone any more, but to get help from anyone willing to
help us!" The aggressive child may respond by accusing the parents
of betrayal and may even claim that distributing the document is in
itself violence. The parents must avoid a discussion of the legitimacy
of their actions, as any such discussion will lead to escalation. The
parents should remember the goal is not to persuade the assailant
they are right but to end the violence.

6. *Reconciliation gestures.* Even in cases of violence against siblings,
the nonviolent resistance should be accompanied by reconciliation
gestures. These are necessary not only to reduce escalation, but
also to show the assailant that he is not ostracized. The parents
continue treating him as their child, who deserves their affection. The combination of curbing the violence and reconciliation

gestures creates the optimal conditions for rehabilitating the aggressor.

The parents of a seventeen-year-old boy sought counseling due to his harsh treatment of his twelve-year-old sister, which had worsened in the last year. The boy would order his sister not to come to the room where he was, and then chase her away with threats and blows when she showed up. At family dinners, when the parents refused to succumb to his demands and insisted the whole family eat together, the boy would kick her under the table. The parents performed several sit-ins in the presence of a relative, but the benefit was short-lived. Increasing the number of relatives involved also brought only short-term relief. The parents wrote a letter describing in detail all the boy's acts of violence toward his sister and gave the boy a copy with a long list of names, including the names of his classmates and their parents, the teachers at school, counselors in his youth movement, and so on. They told him that if he repeated his actions, the report would be sent to everyone on the list. The boy avoided all violence for a few weeks, but then he went back to threatening and hitting, thinking the parents were no longer on alert. The parents sent ten letters and asked the people to call the boy and let him know. The violence ceased. A year-long follow-up showed the violence did not recur and the boy resumed a normal relationship with his sister.

Is that sufficient? Should the victim's trauma and the aggressor's emotional state not also be treated? This question has many answers in professional discourse. A full discussion of them exceeds the present framework, but we would like to reassert that psychological treatment is not the answer to the problem of violence. Likewise, professionals are not to determine in advance that the victim needs to process the trauma psychologically. Such a requirement, when the victim is unwilling, is tantamount to further coercion that reconstructs the passivity and helplessness the victim suffered before (Durrant & Kowalski 1990). Likewise, the aggressor cannot be assumed to require psychological treatment, and surely therapy must not be made a condition of any future benefit (such as a condition for his continuing to live at home). Such a stipulation would render the therapy meaningless.

Measures of nonviolent resistance are meant to end the violence, but they also have therapeutic value: the victim receives documentation and recognition of his suffering, as well as recognition of his right to security. The aggressor receives the experience of parental presence. We must remember that the dominance-oriented child needs, more than anything else, a solid environment to help him channel his energy and restlessness toward legitimate purposes. Restoring parental presence through nonviolent resistance fulfills this role in the best way.

6 CHILDREN WHO TAKE CONTROL
OF THE HOUSE

Of the many parents who approached us to help them deal with their children's aggressive behavior, a subgroup emerged (consisting of about 20 percent of the cases) where the children's aggressiveness was almost never manifested outside the household but was part of their attempt to take control of the house or immure themselves in the "fortress" of their own rooms. Any attempt by the parents to challenge the child's control or self-immurement was met with violence. Most of these children exhibited also obsessive-compulsive disorder (OCD) symptoms or traits.

These violent patterns in children with OCD tendencies have not been described in the professional literature. We think there are two reasons for the professional disregard of this phenomenon. (1) The violence may more easily be kept secret, as it occurs only within the confines of the home, and (2) the prevailing wisdom views compulsive disorders as internalizing rather than externalizing disorders. According to this view, only externalizing disorders become manifest in violent behavior, while internalizing ones are linked to reserved and shy behavior. Violence in children with OCD tendencies shatters this convention, and this might be the reason it has so far eluded professional scrutiny.

CONTROLLING CHILDREN

Children who exhibit this pattern are not violent outside the household at all. In fact, they are usually good students, and sometimes they are socially popular, although some of them are reserved and timid. The common denominator of their behavior outside the family is meticulousness and high performance standards. Sometimes their strictness undermines their functioning, but other times it propels them toward achievements. Within the household, however, this tendency often develops into a system of outrageous demands that infiltrates every area of family life. Any deviation by the parents may be met with the severest punishment. Many of these children also exhibit clear-cut OCD symptoms in areas such as cleanliness, washing, eating, and sleeping rituals. Others exhibit no specific OCD symptoms, but rather more generalized obsessive-compulsive character traits. Thus they demand with the utmost stringency that things be done as they wish, that their personal territory be absolutely inviolable, or that their parents' treatment of them and of their siblings be symmetric to an impossible extent. These demands may be imposed so strictly that the family in fact becomes the executive arm of the child's wishes.

A fifteen-year-old boy imposed on his parents the following sleep ritual: before going to bed he would enter his parents' room and demand that his mother sit down upright, look into his eyes and listen silently to the list of injustices she had committed against him. The boy's speech included curses and obscenities, and went on for about twenty minutes. When it was over the child would go to his room, where he waited for his father. The father would go in, check the window was locked, check the closets and under the bed for terrorists or robbers, and check the bedding for insects. After the boy lay down, the father had to comfort him and sympathize with him for the injustices he had suffered from his mother, concluding with a declaration of enduring love and loyalty. Any disturbance of this order, such as if the mother made a comment, would lead to a violent outburst that might last until the late hours of the night.

A five-year-old girl demanded that her mother join her every evening in checking all the doors and windows in the house. The examination included unlocking and locking each door and window three times, after which the girl or the mother (taking turns) had to pull the window or the door three times to ascertain they were properly locked. The mother then had to turn all of the girl's dolls and stuffed animals toward the wall, while wishing each an individual "good night." Finally, the mother had to tell the girl the same story, always in the same words. If she made a mistake, even of one word, she was required to tell the story all over again.

A twenty-five-year-old college-educated woman forced her parents to give her a detailed report of all the guests they had at home, all the people they visited, and all the phone calls they made. The parents were forbidden to discuss certain subjects or mention certain names. The parents, both working people, had to arrange their schedules so that they could drive her to work and back, a very complicated task, because the daughter's working hours changed every day. When the parents came to therapy this system of rules had been in place for ten years.

A fifteen-year-old boy strictly monitored the volume of his parents' speech. Any deviation from the dictated level, which was close to a whisper, was met with a sharp outburst.

A seventeen-year-old girl made behavior rules for her twelve-year-old brother inside the home: he was not allowed to invite friends over, to listen to music without headphones, or to be in the kitchen or the living room when she was there. When the sister went out of her room, her brother had to immediately go into his room, no matter what he was doing at the time.

A sixteen-year-old boy made strict rules about the use of the family shower. He took a shower first for about two hours, and then each of the other members of the family got seven minutes to shower, in the following order: his brother, his mother, and his father. To make sure they kept to the schedule, he would stand behind the shower door with a stopwatch.

Among the common sanctions for deviations from these rules were shouting and cursing for hours on end, deliberately preventing the parents from sleeping, destroying property, throwing objects, indiscriminately tearing up papers (including scattering the parents' work papers, ripping them, or throwing them out of the window), hiding objects or documents belonging to members of the family, messing up siblings' or parents' closets, hitting, biting, and threatening murder or suicide.

These punishments play a key role in ensuring the parents' unconditional obedience, but they are not the only reason for it. Parents also obey because they are concerned about the child, feel guilty, and believe that they need to make up for the suffering or injustice (real or imagined) they caused him. Moreover, the parents believe the child cannot control his behavior, since it stems from pathological sources. They are afraid that any attempt to resist the symptoms might lead to a mental breakdown or suicide attempt.

Employing Nonviolent Resistance

To prepare parents for nonviolent resistance in these cases, it is necessary first to address several common illusions.

1. The illusion of persuasion and compensation. These children often accuse their parents of having subjected them to severe injustice and deprivation. For instance, they accuse the parents of having always blatantly preferred their siblings to them or, if they are adopted, claim the parents do not treat them as real children. These children's bookkeeping of past injuries sometimes goes back to the day they were born, if not earlier. Their ideal of symmetry and justice is so far reaching that the real world is always found lacking in comparison with their expectations.

The parents' hope that the child might be persuaded of the falseness of her claims or, conversely, that she might be appeased by compensation is illusory. They usually find out to their distress that their best arguments not only fail but seem to reinforce the child's belief in her accusations. The parents' sorrow over the child's sense of deprivation and their feelings of guilt over their own negative reactions to her often lead them into far-reaching compensation attempts. Paying for a trip abroad, buying a motorcycle, and transferring property titles to the child were some of the compensation measures taken by parents we treated. Parental giving is of course a positive thing, but when it is motivated by hope that the sacrifice will win recognition and wipe out the child's grudge, it usually leads to bitter disappointment. For these children, expressing gratitude to their parents would be an intolerable defeat, tantamount to an admission that her struggle was totally unjustified. In none of the cases we treated did the parents' compensation attempts lead to the desired outcome. Instead, their wish to "turn over a new leaf" was flatly rejected, and the parents usually found to their astonishment that their endeavors had led to further escalation. The child usually reacted dismissingly or increased her aggressive behaviors, as if she wanted to prove that "her feelings could not be bought." Often the child was persuaded that if the parents were making such efforts to compensate her, their debts toward her must be even bigger than she thought.

2. The "contract illusion." The parents of these children report repeated attempts to reach agreements or even formal signed contracts with the child to regulate family life. These children's liking for "rational" arguments contributes to the parents' belief that negotiation and the formulation of formal agreements are the way to a solution. This faith, like the previous one, is prone to disappoint. Children who employ obsessive-compulsive control do negotiate not to reach agreement but to reprove their parents and establish their rightness. In their drive to argue, they reject all limiting rules, which are the preconditions of any effective discussion. Every argument with them expands to more and more remote areas, all the way to early childhood. The child thwarts any parental attempt to reach an acceptable solution by opening ancient accounts, for which the parents owe him compound interest. The sense of justice of these children knows no rest, pushing ever harder toward a totally utopian symmetry.

Likewise, the parents' attempts to link benefits to good behavior usually prove futile. For the compulsive controlling child, any external stipulation turns into a power struggle, and any concession on her side becomes a humiliating defeat. In her feeling of being totally in the right, the child will feel justified in cashing all the benefits, keeping her behavior unchanged, and maintaining her belief that the parents are still in her debt.

Understanding this process will enable parents to avoid setting conditions ("I will do this if you do this") that only intensify the child's tendency toward endless bookkeeping. In contrast, if the parents avoid making explicit stipulations, the child's adjustment to the new conditions created by nonviolent resistance will not necessarily be perceived by him as a crushing defeat. Ironically, achievements with these formalistic and argument-loving children usually can be obtained by practical measures that are undertaken without any rational discussion or formalization.

3. The illusion of an imposed or "bought" therapy. The fact that these children's need for control has to do with a specific psychological disorder (OCD) arouses hope that psychotherapy or medication is the key to the problem. Indeed, therapy and medication voluntarily accepted may help the child with OCD. But not so when the therapy is imposed or "bought" by the parents. The following are two typical examples. (1) Parents who caught their son intentionally destroying their property agreed to cancel their demand that the damage be made good, on condition the child agree to have therapy. He gave in, but left the therapy a month later. (2) A divorced mother agreed to cooperate with the rituals her daughter imposed on her during mealtimes and before bed, in exchange for her agreement to take medications. Despite the medical treatment, the daughter's demands intensified. When the mother said she would no longer cooperate with the rituals, the daughter threatened she would stop taking the drugs. The mother, a nurse by profession, said she had acted like the parents of a diabetic child who attempted to buy his cooperation with the medical regime by supplying him with candy!

In such cases, the parents pay a double price: they worsen the home situation and expose themselves to a new threat (that of quitting therapy). Whereas these drawbacks are very clear, the expected benefits of the bought or imposed therapy are highly unclear. Even in cases where the therapy does help ease the OCD symptoms that are centered on the child alone (such as his compulsive washing or checking), this improvement usually has no positive effect on his tendency to control the family. Things are, of course, different when the child goes to therapy voluntarily, without any parental pressure or reward. But even then the parents have to be alert to the possibility that the therapy be turned into a weapon, such as when the child threatens to quit therapy if he does not get his way. In such cases the parents must answer that it is his therapy and that he may leave it if he so wishes.

Parents are advised to abandon the escalating courses of action that follow from those three illusions and convey to the child in words and action the following messages.

That they know they cannot convince the child he is not deprived.

That they cannot compensate him for his feelings of deprivation.

That they cannot correct their past mistakes to his satisfaction.

That they cannot reach an explicit agreement or contract with him to regulate their relationship.

That they cannot control the way he behaves but only influence their own behavior.

That they cannot make him cooperate with psychotherapy or medication.

Overcoming these illusions can help the parents develop an effective program of nonviolent resistance. Then they will operate out of the decision no longer to be passive victims of exploitation and violence, no longer to stand by when siblings are being hurt, and no longer to stay alone with their problem. Parents' expectations in this program are different from the usual expectations of parents of a child with OCD. The goal of nonviolent resistance is not to cure the child but to stop the control. By using nonviolent resistance the focus of the change is transferred to the parents, that is, to ending their capitulation and escalation behaviors. In some of our cases, nonviolent resistance allowed the child to ask for therapy or medication voluntarily later on. Conversely, the parents' capitulation and escalation habits may well stand in the way of any psychotherapy, medication, or even spontaneous improvement in the disorder.

Parents wonder whether the child with obsessive-compulsive tendencies is capable of standing their refusal to cooperate with his demands and rituals. They fear their refusal will lead to a severe worsening of symptoms, to a psychotic breakdown, or even to a suicide attempt. Our experience with such cases shows that these fears do not materialize. The child can be expected to wage a battle for his continued control, but in none of our cases was there evidence of new symptoms, to say nothing of psychotic outbreaks or suicide attempts. On the basis of our experience, we dare assert that the more the parents' capitulate, the stronger the symptoms, and the more the parents resist, the lesser the symptoms. This finding requires elaboration. Perhaps obsessive-compulsive symptoms point to the child's need for clear and binding rules. In the absence of such rules from the outside (i.e., from the parents), the child with such tendencies feels pressed to manufacture them from within. Thus, the parents' capitulation increases the lack of rules and order in the external world, thereby increasing the internal pressure to create an obsessive-compulsive order.

CASE 4: RESISTING THE CHILD'S "IRRESISTIBLE" SYMPTOMS

Larry displayed compulsive behaviors since his early childhood. His parents, Moira and Simon, put him to bed with intricate rituals (a story always told in the same way, covering his body in a certain way, arranging his dolls in the bed in a certain order). There were also complex rituals for meals, and for going to and returning from kindergarten. These tendencies became even more pronounced after his younger brother Danny was born when Larry was four. For years, Larry accused his mother of preferring Danny to him. Simon identified with Larry's pain and felt it was true that Moira favored her younger son over him. The mother did not deny this, but claimed her feelings toward Larry were infected over the years by his demands and his violence.

The parents came for a consultation when Larry was seventeen. His OCD was manifested, among other ways, in his washing for hours a day and in precise rituals before going to school. Larry was treated with medications that significantly reduced the washing and the morning rituals, but brought no relief to the family relations. Larry imposed a long series of rules on his parents and brother and enforced them with threats and rages that sometimes went on late into the night. The list of demands and prohibitions he imposed on his family was comprehensive and strict and made life at home impossible. For example, Larry monitored his parents' phone calls, and any mention of him, even by a hint, led to the immediate disconnection of the phone call. Visits were absolutely forbidden, to both his parents and his brother, with the pretext that the noise disturbed his studying. For the same reason, listening to music or television was allowed only with headphones, while Larry himself listened to music and watched television loudly. Larry's rule also applied to the area of hygiene. The family's washing was strictly scheduled, and the mother was ordered to wash and fold Larry's clothes according to special rules. Larry used each towel only once, and when he finished drying himself he threw it on the floor, which led to heaps of towels accumulating all over the house. The parents had to drive him to school, to after-school activities, and to his individual psychotherapy sessions, since Larry refused to use public transportation, which disgusted him. Another rule forbade the members of the family to serve themselves out of the pots before Larry took his serving. Besides all that, Larry cursed his mother almost every time he saw her. Sometimes, when she was sitting quietly and reading a book, Larry would sneak up behind her and burst into a deafening salvo of curses. He also humiliated his brother frequently. For instance, Larry would stand in his doorway and prevent him from passing through. Of all the members of the family, the father was treated best, but he was also required to maintain complete silence, as were the rest of the family members, so as not to disturb Larry. Moreover, expressions of affection by the father toward other members of the family drew loud protests from Larry. Moira, a physiotherapist, also suffered from interruptions of her work: often Larry burst into her therapeutic sessions, screaming that his brother was disturbing his studying. Moira often lost her temper and shouted and cursed Larry. Sometimes she got physically violent with him.

Larry's condition was a matter of deep dispute between the parents. Simon accused Moira of emotionally rejecting their son, and Moira accused Simon of supporting his violent behavior. Larry efficiently fanned the flames of their dispute and presented his father with a variety of complaints, real or imagined, about Moira's behavior toward him. Despite their disagreements the parents acquiesced to a program of nonviolent resistance against the unceasing demands and the violence. Simon was glad to hear his wife would be required to control her own outbursts as resolutely as she would act against Larry's violence. Moira was glad to hear that her husband would be required to support her struggle against Larry's control and to stop listening to his complaints and accusations against her. Both parents responded positively to the idea of reconciliation gestures. The bridging and uniting value of nonviolent resistance emerged as early as the first meeting. Simon stopped his blind defense of Larry, admitting he really did impose a reign of terror on the household. Simon also admitted that he, too, was violent toward his son, even more frequently than Moira. Moira, in turn, understood that controlling her responses was of crucial importance, not only to guarantee Simon's involvement in the program, but also to prevent escalation. The parents received an instruction manual and were asked to give copies to a few friends and relatives, who were invited to the second therapy session.

This session was attended, besides the parents, by five of their relatives and friends, who were given a detailed description of the goings-on at home. Simon and Moira stated their commitment to avoid any violent action toward Larry. At this session, they decided to stop co-operating with some of Larry's demands, including the prohibition of inviting guests, the demand for complete silence, and the dictates about washing, laundry, eating, and sleeping. The participants each agreed to address Larry separately and tell him that they heard from his parents about what went on in their home, and that the shouting, the threats, the destruction of property, and the harassment of his brother were called "domestic violence." They were also asked to tell Larry that their decision to help his parents stop his violence and his impossible demands did not detract from their positive feelings toward him.

Larry's response was mixed. He was furious at his parent's betrayal in disclosing his private business to people outside the family. He set up meetings with two of the participants outside the home to express his point of view to them. Along with his protest and rage, Larry surprised his parents by adjusting rather easily to their non-cooperation with his prohibitions and demands. The parents could hardly believe their eyes: engrained compulsive demands collapsed overnight, without the appearance of other symptoms and without particular signs of violence.

In some of the problematic behaviors, including verbal abuse of the mother, interruption of her work, and dropping towels, there was no improvement.

The parents wondered whether they should launch a focused campaign on those issues. Another dilemma they faced at the time had to do with a trip overseas, which was promised to Danny as a present for his thirteenth birthday. It was supposed to be a family trip, like one they had taken when Larry reached the same age. Now the parents feared the trip would turn into a trap. They tried to make Larry's participation in the trip conditional on his stopping the violence at home. Simon and Moira demanded a trial week, only after which they would order tickets. Larry controlled himself for two days, but then he went back to assaulting his mother and disrupting her work. Simon and Moira decided a family trip was not possible in those circumstances and wondered whether Moira and Danny should go by themselves. Simon thought that was exactly Larry's nightmare scenario: such a trip would be the final proof of the discrimination of which he had been accusing his mother for years. Simon feared that informing Larry of the trip would generate a crisis, erase all of the achievements, and return the situation back to the beginning or even worse. Moira said that they had no chance of convincing Larry anyway, as his bookkeeping system and demands for symmetry knew no boundaries. She described how Larry's meticulous accountancy documented the precise value of every gift, item of clothing, and outing given to Danny over the years. The parents agreed that an equivalent record of all the good things given to Larry was never made. Moira put an end to the debate by announcing that she refused to give up the trip with Danny (just the two of them) or to accept the veto being imposed by Larry. The parents decided to prepare a "shock absorption plan" for Larry's anticipated reactions.

To everyone's surprise, his reaction was much more moderate than expected. Larry did shout and curse, but no more than usual. The trip went well, Larry and Simon enjoyed each other's company, and the atmosphere at home was good. Larry greeted Moira and Danny's return with screaming, and any mention of the trip was met with door slamming. However, within three days Larry started listening to the stories from the trip and even asked questions. Again, the parents were surprised to discover that breaking Larry's sanctified symmetry did not lead to the expected negative results.

The parents asked for a break in the therapy. They felt there had been a lot of progress and that there was no reason to embark on a new campaign at present. Moira still suffered from verbal abuse and had to continue collecting towels and other objects Larry left in his wake. She also still drove him to school, to his personal therapy, and to other after-school activities. She decided to solve the problem of his bursting into her work sessions by renting an office away from home, which also served to diminish her continuous friction with Larry. Two months later, Moira called and reported a crisis: the violence had increased and Larry had hit her on the head while she was driving, because she refused to lower the radio volume. Simon accused Moira that her trip abroad with Danny had brought on the renewed violence, and Moira went back to accusing

Simon of supporting Larry. Since their first meeting, the parents had not displayed such disparate positions, and this time, as opposed to the first session, the therapist felt that only Moira was prepared to resume nonviolent resistance, while Simon preferred to appease Larry's anger. The therapist informed the couple that the new asymmetric situation required an asymmetric solution. He suggested Moira take a position of "refusing orders" while mobilizing maximum public opinion. The objective was twofold: to stop providing services that were heretofore taken for granted (driving, providing towels, etc.), and to mobilize support against the violence. Moira decided to stop all the driving and to provide Larry with only one towel a day (by putting a lock on the cupboard). She also decided from then on to document every episode of violence and to tell Larry that the description was going to be sent to a list of mutual acquaintances. Simon was told that the cessation of services and the mobilization against the violence would this time be Moira's business, but that his position would have a major impact on the process. It was likely that his moral support for Moira would lead to quick results, whereas supporting Larry would prolong the struggle and might lead to an escalation.

Larry showed again an amazing ability to accept the limits: he made do with one towel a day, his violence dropped dramatically, and for the first time in two years he took a bus. At Simon's initiative, he suggested signing a contract in exchange for resumption of services. Moira said she was no longer interested in contracts of the kind that had been signed in the past. She would resume those services she wanted to provide when she felt sure she was doing this of her own will and not under duress. Larry responded by asking to be sent to a boarding school. Moira replied that the decision to go to a boarding school was his, and that it was up to him to look into possibilities. The boarding school idea was dropped.

Moira did not go back to supplying all the services she had interrupted. Transport was reduced to nearly nothing (most of Danny's rides were also cut off in this process). Towels were still limited to one a day. The violence and the blatant impositions subsided. Larry still cursed and used foul language toward his mother, but his raging outbursts, threats, and enforced sleep deprivation stopped. The family stopped serving as the executive arm of Larry's compulsive drives. Moira summarized the change with these words: "I feel much safer. I know I can defend myself from his control and exploitation, and this gives me space to breathe and to live. My anger toward Larry has also subsided, because I stopped being helpless." This summary signals a substantial change in Moira. Especially promising is the fact that she transferred her attention from Larry's behavior to hers.

In a follow-up session three months later, Moira surprised the therapist with a description of a real improvement in her relationship with Larry. Larry had started expressing his wish to be with her and talk to her, something that was missing from their lives for years. In this case, the nonviolent resistance led not only to stopping the violence and the escalation, but also to more positive relations.

SELF-IMMUREMENT

Compulsive children who display patterns of self-immurement gradually sever their ties with the outside world, and with their parents and family members in particular. Ultimately, they seclude themselves in their rooms, eat alone, and keep themselves busy in their private space. Their parents are denied access to their room. The little communication that there is between them and their parents consists of accusations, shouting, cursing, and sometimes physical violence on the part of the child. The immured child may even reverse day and night, thereby reducing even more the chances of contact.

Self-immurement develops gradually. First, is a diminishing presence at family activities (meals, outings, family events) and at outside activities (school, after-school activities, work, entertainment). Gradually, there is a drop in verbal communication, in some cases to the point of a total break. This is followed by a progressive physical self-seclusion within the room. This situation can endure for years. In all the cases we treated, we found the child's obsessive-compulsive features were present long before the self-immurement began. Ironically, the diagnosis of OCD may often give the parents a feeling of relief, for in most cases they had already consulted professionals and often a diagnosis of schizophrenia was made. The tendency toward diagnosis of schizophrenia stems from the fact that self-immured children tend to develop strange or even bizarre behaviors. We think this bizarreness may result from the combination of OCD and social seclusion. In the absence of social contacts, there is a gradual loss of the need to adjust oneself to accepted norms, so that the obsessive-compulsive tendencies may flourish without restraint. This reflects not necessarily a deeper kind of pathology, but rather the tendency typical to recluses of all kinds, such as monks who took to the desert, self-secluding misanthropes, or prisoners in solitary cells.

As opposed to controlling children, self-immuring children wish not to dictate to their families how to live, but only to be left alone and be provided with their special needs. The relationship between self-immurement and obsessive-compulsive tendencies probably stems from the fact that these children strive for complete control of every detail of their lives, which can be achieved only when life is reduced to a small and protected area on which the outside world cannot encroach. The room of the self-immuring child becomes his kingdom, providing him with the full control to which he aspires.

A girl whose compulsive behaviors related mainly to food stopped attending meals and family events. Gradually, she stopped talking to her mother and father. For two years, she kept on going to school and even began to work. At work she avoided contact with people but did her job well. She gradually abandoned all of her social contacts and spent her free time and weekends in her room. Eventually, she quit her job, reversed her days and her nights, and closeted herself in her room until her parents embarked on a course of nonviolent resistance.

A sixteen-year-old boy began missing school and spent his days recording, sorting, and arranging videotapes. For this purpose he needed thirty new videotapes each week, which were provided by his parents. No one was allowed to enter his room. The walls of the house, which began filling with videotapes, were also off-limits for the other members of the family. He reduced his verbal contact with both parents until it stopped completely. Particularly severe restrictions were placed on the mother: she was not allowed to walk past his room or go near the video shelves in the other rooms. Every time she got near one of the forbidden places, he would shout at her or throw something at her. For a while he stayed in touch with a few friends and talked to them on his cellphone for hours a day. When the parents protested over the phone bill, he put the phone outside his room and severed all interpersonal contacts.

Employing Nonviolent Resistance

In cases of self-immurement, the child's complete dependence on her parents is obvious. The protected kingdom could not survive for even one day without the parents' acquiescence and provisioning. The main rule, whose violation would make the whole self-immuring project crumble, is the sanctity of the territory. This sanctity consists of the prohibition of entering and the prohibition of making any changes. Addressing these prohibitions is at the heart of the nonviolent resistance program against self-immurement.

The territorial nature of self-immurement lends the sit-in special potency. Whereas its use against other forms of aggression is a means of promoting the child's gradual adaptation to the parents' resolve, in cases of self-immurement, the very act of sitting in the child's room affects the phenomenon's survival conditions. A room in which parents are sitting is no longer the child's fortress! Already after the first sit-in, the room begins to fill with signs of parental presence. If the parents also do some straightening up while they are in the room, then both of the two prohibitions that keep the self-immurement effective (the prohibition against entry and the prohibition against making changes) are violated. In one of the cases we treated, the salient sign of the parents' entrance was the vary havoc created by the child as a protest against their presence (he threw all his books at the parents and turned out the closet and the shelves). The mother later on helped him rearrange the room, a gesture of reconciliation that further changed the conditions of the boy's self-immurement.

The very potency of the sit-in in these cases deters many parents, who are afraid their child will collapse, run away from home, or commit suicide. These fears may lead them to prefer tolerating things as they are. It is then important to present them with arguments against their continuing surrender. One is that the ongoing self-immurement will lead to serious damage to the child's development: life stops, fear of the outside world grows, the sense of helplessness deepens, and the self-image worsens. For all this, it is the continued immurement and not its challenge by the parents that actually puts the child in danger. Indeed, we know of cases of self-immured children who ended by committing suicide (none of these cases were in our treatment). On the other hand, of the many cases we treated, there was not one case of suicide attempt or mental breakdown, and in the one case in which the child ran away from home, he was out for only two hours. We must remember that nonviolent resistance conveys a message not only of resistance, but also of parental presence. The parents are actually saying: "We are here." Their reappearance on the scene reduces the child's loneliness and thereby militates against the danger of suicide.

Parents who were persuaded to act against the immurement need not only encouragement, but also practical help to deal with their fears. The best way to do so is to help the parents get prepared for the child's possible reactions. Thus parents should prepare in advance a supportive network to help them face the escalation and give them and the child the feeling that they are not alone. Laying out the net allows also for mediation, which may be of critical importance in rebuilding their lives after the immurement ends.

CASE 5: A GENTLE SIT-IN

Thirteen-year-old Zack's seclusion was established very gradually, almost without confrontations. His parents, Dina and Joe, recalled a brief period of attrition at the beginning, when they had tried resisting his increasing absences from school. Their conclusion from those clashes (featuring shouting, a refusal to get out of bed, and a growing avoidance of them) was: "This is the wrong way to work with Zack. It is only making things worse!" Since then the parents avoided any attempts to present Zack with forceful demands. Everything had to be achieved by dialogue and agreement. Zack, too, was very keen in avoiding conflicts: when he still went to school he would stay home for a few days after every small conflict he had in class. Both parents believed his aversion to conflicts (which reflected their own) was evidence that conflicts might be deeply damaging for him. The parents came for counseling after Zack had been home for about a year. He had severed his ties with his friends, reversed day and night, and spent most of his time in his room, reading or at the computer.

Zack showed signs of OCD from the age of seven, when his little brother was born. He was physically averse to the baby, avoided touching things his brother had touched (claiming he had slobbered on everything), and even stayed away from places where the infant's presence was obvious. Joint meals were possible only if a number of taboos were strictly observed. His aversion to his brother also served as a justification for Zack to lock his room, for his brother's entrance would contaminate it. Over the years Zack's fears of contamination expanded: he washed his hands dozens of times a day and took long showers, sometimes for hours at a time.

Both parents were equally committed to the principle of gentle persuasion. They both had very negative memories of their attempts to establish facts unilaterally. They said it had taken months to restore their relationship with their son after the confrontations. On the other hand, their patient persuasion had borne fruit: family meals, for instance, were resumed after an interval following a series of discussions and compromises. Also, the discussions allowed intimacy, and the very act of persuasion created a feeling of closeness. In the matter of going to school and staying home, persuasion had been a total failure, but the parents doubted any other method would have been more successful.

As his seclusion deepened, Zack began avoiding his parents, too. This development made the parents fear the seclusion could be as dangerous to him and to the family as the confrontations, and caused them to consider a new approach. After a few sessions in our program of nonviolent resistance, they became willing to conduct sit-ins focused on Zack's school avoidance. Their fear of conflicts led them to soften the sit-in procedure and modify it. They decided that if Zack wanted to leave the room, they would let him, but they would stay there. In this way Joe and Dina designed their own version of a sit-in, in which a gentle determination replaced the grim determination that is more typical of the procedure. This form of sit-in turned out to be quite effective. Zack took advantage of his right to leave the room, but since this prevented him from staying in his room, the parents gradually achieved their goal. After three weeks of gentle sit-ins Zack went back to school, but only on half of the days, and only at 11 A.M. (because of his difficulty in waking up and his prolonged washing rituals). The parents, however, felt Zack had taken a very significant step.

The connection between the compulsive symptoms and the tardiness and absences from school reopened the debate over medical treatment. The psychiatrist who had examined Zack a year earlier thought medication could relieve his compulsive symptoms and social anxieties, but the idea was dropped because of Zack's opposition. Joe undertook sitting at the computer with Zack to gather information about OCD and social anxiety and also about available medical treatments. This activity was enjoyable for Zack, who loved to surf on the Internet, enjoyed his father's company, and appreciated intellectual discourse. Zack showed impressive skill at detecting negative data about the medications, but Joe showed him this information lacked research support and was spread mainly by militant antipsychiatric groups. After one month of joint sittings, Zack remained as opposed to the medication as at the beginning.

During this time Joe and Dina began attending a parents' support group. At one meeting Joe presented his attempts to lead Zack to accept medical treatment. The members of the group argued that the process of verbal persuasion had proven ineffective. When Joe and Dina asked what they thought the alternative was, since a child could not be forced to take medicine, a member said: "Sit down in his room and say: 'Here is the pill and here is the water! I am not going out until you take it!'" That option, which was definitely irrelevant to Dina and Joe before, became practicable when the group stood behind them. Later Joe shared that when he showed up in Zack's room with the pill and the water, he felt as if his voice sounded different, "as if the group was speaking out of my mouth." He told Zack: "We are done gathering data. You have OCD and, as a father, I can not go on living without doing everything possible to treat the disorder. I will not leave this room until you take this pill!" Joe sat in the room for an hour and a half and refused to get into any argument. Zack did not take the pill. Finally Joe got up and left, with the intention of coming back later, leaving the glass and the pill behind. When he came back an hour later he found the pill gone and the glass empty. The next day Zack took the pill in front of his parents. From there on Zack fully cooperated with the medical treatment.

These events led Joe and Dina to reexamine the idea of verbal persuasion. With the help of the therapist and the group, they redefined Zack's problem. They realized Zack suffered from a lack of internal structure and rules, and especially ways to begin and end activities. This deficiency led to a blurring and "dragging" of his daily schedule, on the one hand, and the invention of arbitrary rules (the compulsive rites) to fill the gap, on the other hand. In this situation, the parents' reliance on verbal persuasion actually deprived Zack of the feeling of a clear external reality, and thereby aggravated his inner lack of structure. This formulation led the parents to decide to provide Zack from then on with a clear-cut structure that would help him get up in the morning and go to school. They would get up early in the morning, about an hour and a half before their usual time, to wake up Zack and get him to leave for school on time. The parents were willing to even dress him, as long as he got to school on time. They did not believe Zack would fight with them; at the very most he would resist them passively.

Zack reacted as expected. For one month the parents felt they were dressing up a lifeless body. Zack fully awoke only when they got close to his school. A few times he asked to take a shower in the morning, which made him a few hours late for school. With the group's support, the parents put a stop to the morning showers. Throughout the entire period Dina and Joe had not raised their voices or struggled with Zack physically. Gently but with admirable tenacity they woke him up, dressed him, and even carried him into the car. There was one positive sign that encouraged them: when he got to school, Zack gladly joined its activities. Gradually, he started participating in the morning preparations, and after two months of hard work he dressed himself and took the school bus. His scholastic progress was very quick and within a short time he closed a big gap. Three months after the morning program began, Zack brought friends home for the first time. This signaled the end of his self-immurement.

7 PARENTS AND TEACHERS: THE VITAL ALLIANCE

There are close parallels between the situation of parents and teachers regarding children with behavior problems: (1) the child's behavior problems at home are often reconstructed at school; (2) parents and teachers base their authority on the same foundations; and (3) the expectations from parents and teachers (and the criticisms against them) are similar. In addition, the tasks of both parties are so inter-dependent that it would be hard for either one to succeed without the other's support. Nonetheless, relations between parents and teachers are often extremely strained (Uziel 2001).

One might venture that of all the parties that affect the parental effort, the child's teachers and school are the most important. Suffice it to mention there is no other place in which the child spends as many hours and years as the school. Concurrently, the parents are the school's chief source of support in dealing with the child's behavior problems. Any teacher knows that a negative parental attitude toward the school can badly aggravate a child's behavior problems. Therefore, an attempt by either party to curb the child's aggressive behavior without the other's support – or worse, with its resistance – is like trying to build a dam with a sieve.

FACTORS THAT WEAKEN THE AUTHORITY OF PARENTS AND TEACHERS

Several processes in modern society undermine the authority of parents and teachers. Among them are the weakening of the familial and communal ties due to living conditions in crowded and anonymous cities, the rapid obsolescence of adults' knowledge as the result of modernization processes, and the permissive ideology that leads many adults to willingly abdicate their authority. These processes have far-reaching implications.

The Isolation of the Parent and the Teacher

In the last hundred years, the number of divorces and of single-parent families in the Western world has sharply increased. At the same time, ties with the extended family have greatly weakened. As a result, many parents are much more isolated than in previous generations. Research shows that the child of a single parent is at a high risk of exhibiting behavior problems. This vulnerability declines, however, if the parent is supported by members of the extended family (Dornbusch et al. 1985; Steinberg 1987). Parental isolation is also affected by socio-communal factors. For instance, the frequency of behavior problems in children whose parents are not well integrated in the community (e.g., immigrants without a support group) is considerably higher. Parental isolation is further exacerbated by the high value set on privacy in the modern world, which makes parents reluctant to disclose their problems with their children.

Teachers, too, are isolated, by definition. The teacher stands alone in front of a class and is expected to deal with the problems by herself. Even though this has always been the case, the problem has worsened in the last generations: in the past, the teacher's sense of belonging within a small community where she was personally known by most of the people was much clearer than it is today in a big school in a modern, anonymous city. The teacher's feeling of being alone is further sharpened by the fashionable criticisms directed at the teaching profession. In face of these criticisms, the teacher may choose to hide the acute problems she has in her class, since disclosing them might be viewed by her critics as further evidence of her failure. This, just as in the case of parents, deepens the teacher's isolation and vulnerability, contributing to the problem's perpetuation.

Considering the serious pressures they face, teachers could have been expected to develop mutual support mechanisms. Unfortunately, mutual support among teachers usually exists only as a spontaneous and not as an organized phenomenon. Moreover, alongside the spontaneous help there is often also stiff competition among the teachers, a process that increases the teacher's sense of isolation. Lack of mutual help among teachers is further abetted by the widely accepted view that a teacher's authority is very much a personal attribute, an unexplainable charisma that some teachers have and others lack. In a program we designed to encourage teachers to cooperate within the school, we noticed a tendency of the more established and stronger teachers to convey the message that serious discipline problems "could never happen in their class." Supposedly, only those teachers who lacked the "right stuff" suffered from these problems. In such an atmosphere, many teachers would prefer not to disclose their difficulties, since revealing them would be tantamount to admitting they did not have "what it takes." Viewing a teacher's authority as stemming from personal charisma ignores the weighty contribution of systemic factors, chief among them the support the teacher receives.

There is a similar attitude toward parents. Certain parents are perceived as having "authority" and "parental instincts," while others are perceived as lacking them. Here, too, systemic factors are ignored, such as the parent's isolation or harsh environmental conditions. The idea that it all depends on the parent's personal profile often leads to attempts by social services to remove the child from the home or to provide him with a parental substitute. This attitude leads parents, just like teachers, to prefer to keep their problems secret, rather than risk public exposure. Thus a trap is set up, whereby the very disclosure of the problem, which is a condition for receiving help from the outside, threatens to increase criticism and provide evidence of the parents' or teacher's inadequacy. No wonder that parents and teachers may prefer to remain silent, even at the price of perpetuating their vulnerability.

Sabotage of the Parent's and Teacher's Authority

Serious conflicts between the parents can fatally damage parental authority (Omer 2000). When parents blame each other ("You are a rejecting father!" "You are ruining the child!"), when one party tries to get around or cancel the other's decisions, or when one party tries to form an alliance with the child at the other's expense, parental presence is mutually neutralized, and the child's aggressive and self-damaging behaviors increase.

Parties outside the nuclear family may also undermine parental authority. For instance, when a grandfather showers the children with money and gifts to the point that they disdain parental giving or when a grandmother provides her granddaughter with a refuge every time she has a conflict with her mother, the parents' authority is sabotaged. Even therapists may inadvertently undermine parental authority, such as when therapeutic confidentiality turns into a mantle to cover up an adolescent's destructive behavior or when therapy turns into a parent-blaming ritual. The therapy then provides the child with ammunition for his destructive struggle.

Cooperation between parents and teachers is a key element in strengthening each other's authority, whereas mutual alienation invariably weakens it. A particularly bad situation arises when the parties stop talking to each other. A breakdown of communications seriously hurts the teacher, because the parent becomes a party who not only condones but also unwittingly encourages the child's misbehavior (e.g., by becoming one-sidedly receptive to the child's complaints against the teacher, no matter how far-fetched they may be). Ironically, the parent who does this is also undermining her own authority, because the breakdown of relations means the teacher stops updating her about the child's behavior. The parent thus remains in the dark about all school occurrences, a process that inevitably weakens parental presence (Loeber & Dishion 1984; Loeber & Stouthamer-Loeber 1986). It is not surprising that children with negative leanings try to gain leeway for their activities by furthering the break-off of relations between parents and teachers.

The Permissive Ideology

"Authority" has become a dirty word in the Western world, especially when it comes to child rearing. The permissive ideology peaked in the 1960s and 1970s, when the prevailing belief was that the ideal education is achieved in conditions of total acceptance and freedom and in an environment with no demands or boundaries. The expectations from this approach to child rearing were almost utopian in scope: children would grow up free, curious, creative, confident, sociable, and nonviolent. These high hopes were disproved in a long series of studies that found that raising children without boundaries or authority, even if done in a loving and accepting atmosphere, leads to a lowering of achievements and a rise in violence, drugs, sexual promiscuity, and delinquency. In addition, children who grew up in homes with a permissive ideology had lower self-images than children who grew up in more authoritative households (Baumrind 1971, 1991; Eisenberg & Murphy 1995).

Despite this evidence, the very need to employ formal authority is still viewed by many as an indictment. The prevailing assumption remains that if the parent or teacher were sensitive and acceptant enough to the child's needs, the problems would not have arisen. This assumption turns the dialogue between parent and teacher into a litigation where each side accuses the other of insensitivity and lack of empathy toward the child. Under the surface, the opposite expectation, that the other side assume the unpopular authoritative role, also is active. Thus teachers expect parents to call their child to order, and parents expect the teacher to be strict. Both sides thus blame and are blamed on opposite counts: a failure of acceptance and empathy, on the one hand, and a failure of authority, on the other.

The abdication of authority roles regarding children is one of the amazing features of modern society. In almost all known cultures, adults have asked themselves how they could fulfill their guiding and restraining role more effectively. In modern Western society, in contrast, adults ask, perhaps for the first time in history, how they could best relinquish those authority roles! In this atmosphere, it is expected that parents and teachers will sound hesitant, since the very use of a determined voice is viewed as proof of their failure.

Criticism of Parents and Teachers

Parents and teachers are among the most widely criticized groups in society. Complaints about parents appear all the time in widely read popular psychology books. Criticism of teachers abounds in the press and in public discourse, and among its avid consumers are, of course, parents. The contents of the criticism are similar: both are accused of failing to raise children who are intelligent, curious, or endowed with positive values and emotional health. Teachers are also accused of failing to transmit knowledge.

Parents (mainly mothers) have been held responsible for enormous damages, such as making their children dependent, anxious, depressive, perverse, autistic, and schizophrenic. These statements remain widely accepted, no matter how much they are refuted by research. Like other scapegoats, parents are constantly accused of "poisoning" the child's soul. Such books as *Toxic Parents* (1989) ride the wave of this belief and support it in turn.

This view is not limited to popular books with a simplistic approach. Books that are highly valued by professionals, such as Alice Miller's *The Drama of the Gifted Child* (1981) present very similar ideas. In Miller's book, the destruction of the child's primal innocence is caused by the parents' betrayal: the parents' excellence fantasies about the child are poison for her soul, causing her to deny herself and become a tool for the parents' satisfaction. The only hope, according to Miller, is to raise the consciousness of enlightened witnesses, who will be ready to reveal to children their parents' hidden cruelty toward them, thus allowing them to free themselves before it is too late. "The drama of the gifted child" has become the bible of many parent-bashers. Sometimes parents become "self-bashers" when reading the book. Thus a woman who was six months' pregnant came to me for counseling and said she was considering having an abortion, because reading Miller's book convinced her she was going to exploit her child and destroy her soul. In this case, even before the child was born the mother already placed herself in the accused bench. The paralyzing influence that these beliefs would have on her future parenthood can only be imagined.

The offensive against teachers in public discourse is no less sweeping. In a rare defense of teachers, one Israeli journalist wrote: "There is hardly a profession treated with such contempt and hatred as teaching. The average teacher is depicted as an ugly lady with a shrill voice, suffering from mild to moderate mental retardation. The contemporary teacher is portrayed as a latter-day female bogeyman with facial hair."

This derision is just the tip of the iceberg. Teachers' intentions, features, and influence are often presented in a highly negative light. Teachers are accused of caring about nothing but their salaries and holidays ("Which other profession has such holidays? They should be sent to teach in old-age homes and in prisons!"), of being of low professional ability ("Anyone can teach!"), devoid of intellectual or personal skills ("What level of people go to teachers' college?"), lazy ("She just crosses the door into the classroom and tells the kids to start doing their workbooks. That's all she does!"), and devoid of a sense of mission ("Where are the teachers of yore?"). As to their influence, teachers are accused of complete impotence, on the one hand, and of the ability to thoroughly destroy a child's soul, on the other ("Schools extinguish every spark of creativity!") (Katznelson 2001).

These negative attitudes are not the exception but the rule. In a study of the mutual attitudes of parents and teachers in Israel, thirty randomly selected parents were interviewed about their attitudes toward teachers (Uziel 2001). Most displayed deep contempt and hostility. The following are some examples.

My son is gifted but dysgraphic. When the class was learning how to write, he couldn't cope and started acting out. His teacher scolded, criticized, and teased him with no end before his classmates. Things got worse and worse. She knew about his dysgraphia but didn't care and she always flew out of the classroom as soon as the bell rang.

The boy writes stories and poems, and when he brought them to the class she said disbelievingly: "Where did you copy this from?" She refused to believe he wrote it. At this age the teacher is like a god. The boy assumed she must be right about him. His situation deteriorated into serious physiological and social problems.

In this passage the teacher is described as small-minded and selfish ("she 'flies' out of class as soon as the bell rings"), totally insensitive ("where did you copy this from?"), and as being possessed of an almost supernatural ability to cause damage ("It deteriorated into serious physiological and social problems"). Even if there is some truth in the mother's report, there has obviously been no attempt to hear the teacher's side of the story. The teacher is so described that one might have suspected she "flew out" of the classroom on a broomstick.

My child's teacher wanted to encourage the kids to do homework, and hung a list of the children who did it on the classroom door for everyone to see. We parents came and said she couldn't humiliate the children in public. It fosters unhealthy competition and can castrate the children. This teacher has no personality and no brains. She refused to budge. Finally we managed to get rid of her.

Even without agreeing with the teacher's method, it is hard to see it as a public humiliation of children. The presumed psychological ramifications ("it can castrate them") are highly unreasonable. The exaggerated description leads to an exaggerated reaction: the furious parents "managed to get rid of her." The phrase "get rid of the teacher" recurred in many interviews in parents' descriptions of their intentions or actions.

My child is an individualist and has strong opinions. The class was discussing the concept "man is superior to beast." The teacher did not accept his interpretation of the phrase and they got into an argument. She could not deal with him and threw him out of the classroom. He is a strong child, and on the way out he laughed in her face. We asked for a meeting with the principal and the teacher, but she refused to budge on her position, insisting that he was the one "who was impertinent."

This is a typical event in the parent-teacher-child triangle: following an argument between the child and the teacher, the child behaved in a manner (not described by the mother) that led the teacher to remove him from the classroom. His response to being removed ("he laughed in her face") is described by the mother with obvious pride. The parents call a confrontation meeting with the principal, but the teacher "insists" that the child is "impertinent."

My son, a child who went through three schools, who has trouble accepting authority, finally got out of the army too. He is very smart but does not study. One of his teachers was a bad high school teacher so she was transferred to an elementary school. She had no educational abilities and she never asked me for any information about him. We, the parents, organized against her and got her thrown out. With another new teacher he had daily clashes. She could not deal with it, she was unable to control the class and she did not know the children. Two weeks after she came I got the principal to move him to another class. He is a special child and the teachers do not know how to deal with him, to make it interesting for him. The teachers are rotten – every one of them.

In this case the mother admits the child has a problem, but her descriptions of the teachers ("the teachers are rotten – every one of them"), and the actions she initiated (getting the teacher "thrown out") would guarantee that any attempts to establish some kind of parent-teacher cooperation would fail.

My daughter and her friends worked hard and with my husband prepared a detailed model illustrating a principle in biology. When they brought it to class, the teacher disqualified it, claiming they didn't follow the instructions she had given. The girls were very hurt, especially my daughter, who felt responsible because of her father's guidance. When we asked the teacher for an explanation, she refused. Finally, my husband intervened by talking to the teacher and the supervisor. They accepted the project and gave it a reasonable grade, not before beating any trace of enthusiasm for biology out of the children. Probably the teacher felt threatened because she is an immigrant and is having trouble with the language. But the damage was done. A few weeks later the project was presented in a journal for teaching science!

Emphasizing the teacher's immigrant status is no accident. In many reports, parents described teachers by placing them in an inferior reference group from their point of view ("old," "young," "foreign," "woman"). In this passage the teacher is repeatedly deprecated: the message is that the girl (with her father's help) is much better than her teacher. Along with her complete devaluation, the teacher is also depicted as possessed of a tremendous power of destruction. She is someone who has the ability to "beat any trace of enthusiasm for biology" out of the children in one fell swoop. This joining of devaluation with attributions of negative power comes up in many parents' descriptions of teachers. Thus the teacher becomes a witch: weak and inferior by nature, but highly destructive in her powers.

My twelve-year-old son is a straight-A student. He dislikes his grammar teacher because she is very old and has old-fashioned ideas and methods. One day they had a fierce argument about something they were studying and at the end the teacher claimed the boy was impudent. The boy was sent to the library as a punishment. I was called in by the principal to support the teacher before my son, but refused. I told the teacher point-blank that she was intolerant and punitive. She said it was because of parents like me, who do not educate their children, that children are like that today. I told her my boy is sharp and she has to deal with kids like him.

Here we witness how the mother's support of her "sharp" son and his outspoken attack against the teacher can work as an incitement for the boy's aggressive behavior.

My son went up to the math teacher at the end of class and she ignored him. When he tried to talk to her again she called him a "nuisance." Of course, he was hurt and recoiled. We sent the teacher a letter and she did not respond. We called the principal and she called us right back. The teacher lied and said my son went up to her at the beginning of the class rather than the end. We met the principal and she reprimanded the teacher in front of us. She seems to have learned the lesson and improved the way she treats the kids since then, but I think she is doing it because she is afraid the children will go to their parents. She even tells the kids: "Don't tell your parents!"

Here the teacher is described as inconsiderate, lying, and devious. She does not even get credit for changing her behavior in the desired direction: she did it only out of fear. The example ends with a further indictment: the teacher is depicted like a child begging not to be informed on.

Though we do not mean to justify the actions attributed to the teachers in these examples, we must keep in mind that the descriptions are the result of a double filter: first by the child and then by the parent. One can only imagine what things would look like from the teacher's standpoint. In these descriptions, the teachers are invariably maligned, while the children are glorified or commiserated with for the supposed damage they suffered. The accompanying parental actions (throwing out the teacher or demanding an apology meeting) are of course not at all helpful. Turning the teacher into a worthless and destructive figure that should be harassed by all possible means necessarily leads to a breakdown in the relations. The child's behavior can then only become worse.

The stereotypical view of the teacher and the school in these examples involves a number of thought-provoking contradictions.

1. *The teacher's power.* The teacher is omnipotent in her ability to harm and powerless in her ability to educate or impart knowledge. Thus schools are commonly imputed with the power of destroying the child's mental faculties. On this view, children come to school open, curious, and with sparkling eyes but are gradually "educated" into becoming bored and apathetic conformists. Teachers are also

viewed as commonly injuring the individual child's soul: the coldness, insults, and formality they exude stand in sharp contrast to the
warmth and the love the child receive at home: "At age six, smiling,
active, curious and happy children enter the impervious system and
the crushing competition machine... children nurtured on boundless human warmth are received with stinging coldness."[1]

Hand in hand with their boundless power to harm, teachers are
viewed as totally powerless: they are incapable of controlling the
class, preventing violence, and overcoming children's slightest problems in understanding the material.

2. *The goal of school.* While schools are expected to demonstrate
maximum efficiency and a competitive ability to impart knowledge
(e.g., in preparation for college-entry exams), they are also blamed for
having become grade factories. In fact, teachers are expected to fulfill
both goals at once: improve the product (the grades) and deepen
personal attention. If the teacher focuses on one of the goals, she
is criticized for neglecting the other. Usually the teacher is criticized
from both directions, and often by the same parents.

3. *The teacher's authority.* The teacher should "keep the class on a
short lead," but only with the gentlest means; he should make the
children work hard, but only through personal charisma. Parents
often justify these expectations by their nostalgic memories of their
own childhood teachers. The idealization of the teachers of the past
emerged in almost all the interviews with parents: these were teachers
with a sense of mission, spontaneously authoritative, and contagious
in their enthusiasm. That ideal teacher, who resides in the parent's
heart, becomes a yardstick by which the teacher of today is harshly
judged. It is no wonder that in the comparison, today's teachers lose
hands down. The gap can be explained by our tendency to glorify
the past and to be selective in our memories (the ideal teacher of
the past was of course the exception and not the rule), as well as the
fact that the parents looked up to the teachers of yore as children,
while they often look down at their children's present teachers. The

---

[1] Quoted from a letter to the Israeli newspaper *Haaretz*.

question of whether the quality of teaching has declined over the years is complex and cannot be separated from such issues as class size or population changes. Beyond these social processes, the unfair comparison is deeply tainted by nostalgic longings. After all, we all know that life is not what it used to be, the world is not what it used to be, kids aren't what they used to be, and in the immortal words of Simone Signoret, even nostalgia is no longer what it used to be.

The conflicting expectations as to the teacher's authority have serious implications: the teacher has to control without controlling, stop without brakes, and protect without support. Woe is the teacher, for instance, who does not report a child's violence. On the other hand, woe is she whose report reaches the police or becomes public knowledge, thus placing a lifelong stigma on the problematic child. The teacher saddled with conflicting expectations has to know that if serious problems occur in her class, she can expect a public lynching. In a shocking case of collective rape in an Israeli high school, the school itself became the butt of an unprecedented media offensive. A long series of venomous newspaper articles denounced the school and turned it into the main villain in the story. And this happened even though a commission of inquiry determined that it was school officials who discovered the crime, reported it to the authorities, informed the parents, and offered the support they could to the injured girl. Among the measures that some of the school critics suggested as interventions that could have prevented the rape were showing the whole school a play that deals with teen-age sex, teaching a program about battered women and, giving preventive psychotherapy beforehand to the rapists and the victim. Unfortunately, anyone who knows even a little of the copious research literature about children's violence will realize how futile are these solutions.

RESTORING THE PARENT-TEACHER ALLIANCE

Public awareness of the scope of violence in schools today provides an opportunity for parents and teachers to examine their relationship and restore their alliance. Whereas in the last decades, parents

often increased their involvement in the schools in the role of critics, sometimes even using threats (militant parent committees sometimes issued warnings to specific teachers that they were "under close
observation," backing the warnings with the names of teachers they
had already "thrown out"), today a very different relationship can
be built, since many parents are open to the message of working together to make schools safer. In our lectures to parents at schools, we
have found them receptive to the idea that their attitudes of hostility toward the teacher weaken the teacher's authority and empower
the violent children. The parents understand well that there can be
no vacuum of authority in school: weakening the teacher creates an
empty space that is quickly filled by the more aggressive children.
Parents understand that threats on their part lead teachers to pur-
sue a strategy of minimal reporting. Parents also react positively to
the idea that restoring the teacher's authority will not only increase
their children's security but also improve their learning conditions.
A teacher that has no support or is being threatened will have a hard
time maintaining order in the classroom. Under such conditions, the
study environment is inevitably subverted.

Parents and teachers respond positively to the idea of employing a
joint strategy of nonviolent resistance against violent behaviors. The
teacher has a paramount interest in such an alliance: parents are the
teacher's main potential supporters and provide the most important
basis of public opinion toward the school. The parents, too, have
a clear interest in restoring the alliance, since it not only improves
the security and quality of teaching at school, but also helps them
deepen their presence in the child's life.

Even though conditions are ripe, the parent-teacher alliance will
not restore itself spontaneously. Years of suspicion, ingrained habits
of mutual criticism, and the temptation to take action against disappointing teachers make the transition difficult. Systematic work will
be needed to persuade principals, teachers, parent committees, and
parents at large. Some practical ideas are listed below that can help
prevent escalation or communication breakdown between parents
and teachers.

1. *Improving ways of addressing each other.* Parents and teachers often address each other in ways viewed as critical, accusatory, and demanding. The following are examples of statements that make parents feel immediately attacked.

> Please come to school next Tuesday to discuss your son's violence.
>
> I want to let you know that your son does not do his homework.
>
> I want to inform you that your daughter does not attend school regularly.
>
> Your son has serious discipline problems.

Such curt addresses cannot but arouse parental resistance. Most parents feel that disparaging their child equals disparaging themselves. Feeling that the address constitutes an attack on the child, they see it as their duty to come to the child's defense.

Parents are usually no more tactful toward the teachers. A common kind of damaging address is to openly attack the teacher about an injustice that she putatively committed against the child. A particularly negative ritual is when the parents ask for a meeting with the principal to pressure the teacher into a formal apology. The parent may leave such a meeting with a triumphant smile, but at a high price: serious damage has been done to any chance of future cooperation. In addition, a drop in the level of the teacher's reporting about the child can be expected.

Another negative element in the way parents and teachers address each other is the mutual assumption that the other is wholly responsible for the problem's solution. For instance, teachers look to parents to make their children stop coming late, stop misbehaving, and do their homework regularly, while parents look to teachers to curb the child's behavior problems and improve his concentration and his social standing in the class. Surely, it is legitimate to hope the other can do these hard jobs. There is nothing wrong with hoping. It is the assumption that these are the other's unquestionable duties that is misplaced.

We must remember that when it comes to children with behavior problems, parents and teachers often feel equally helpless. Each side knows that it cannot do what is expected of him alone. The message from the other party that succeeding in these complex goals is their basic responsibility is taken as an accusation and a demand to do the impossible. No wonder the party who feels attacked will choose a strategy of counterattack.

New ways of mutual address must be developed. Each side should let the other know she is seeking his help to improve her own effectiveness in dealing with the child. Each side should let the other know she would be glad to help him achieve the common goals. Each side should let the other know that it would be hard for each of them alone to succeed but that if they cooperate, the chances of success will increase. In simple words, a mutual-help working alliance should be offered. Each side should stress his own commitment to improving his own performance, offer the other help (such as in reporting, coordinating steps, and building a common program), and emphasize the need to get out of the isolation. These messages should be devoid of all demanding or accusing undertones. In this way, the chances will be maximized of breaking free from defensiveness, disconnection, and escalation.

2. *Doing "respect work."* Far from being merely a cliché, the issue of mutual respect between parents and teachers deserves serious and practical consideration. We need to work at our ability to respect for the simple reason that our habits of thinking and reacting have brought us to the opposite extreme, where disrespect has become almost second nature. It does not suffice to understand that our negative opinions are flawed and destructive. We must inoculate ourselves against the negative stereotypes, thus becoming able to convince the other party we have abandoned the insulting positions we held in the past and have adopted new, constructive ones.

"But what if I do not respect her? Am I supposed to pretend I respect her?" the distraught mother or teacher asks. The assumption behind such questions is that respect is a spontaneous feeling. In fact, this is not the case. Respect is the result of self-work. Feelings of respect arise when we are willing to doubt our instant negative judgments. Statements such as "All the teachers want is more holidays and money!" "Anyone can be a teacher!" "The child is wild because his parents are like that too!" or "The parents want to dump their problems on us!" reflect anger and helplessness and not an objective reality. The great majority of parents and teachers have honest good intentions, even if they are unable to carry them out. Teaching and parenting are very hard jobs that require the utmost efforts. "Respect work" is the effort to relinquish our disparaging attitudes, developing instead the habit of looking at the other with empathy for his efforts, pains, good intentions, and partial achievements.

The following ideas may help perform this "respect work." (1) The other side is sovereign in his territory (the teacher in the classroom and the parent at home); (2) the other side is having just as hard a time as we are in dealing with the child with behavior problems; (3) we may get help from them, just as they may get help from us; and (4) we are both in the same boat, and will either sink or swim together.

Parents and teachers have to work at these ideas, translating them into practical terms. Both sides will then feel the other party appreciates their efforts and troubles. Under these conditions the pronoun "we" may denote a new togetherness, replacing the accusing "you." If the effort of performing "respect work" does not seem worth our bother, we must remember the alternative is very pernicious: a decline of both the parent's and the teacher's authority and a further deterioration in the child's behavior.

3. *Agreeing on nonviolent resistance as a common platform.* Just like nonviolent resistance serves as a bridge between parents with different approaches, it can help to be a bridge between the attitudes of parents and teachers, helping them to define common goals and strategies, to mutually assign the respective roles in the joint effort, and to evolve a common language acceptable to both. In all these respects, nonviolent resistance provides an ideal platform for restoring the parent-teacher alliance.

4. *Applying the principle of openness.* This principle affects mainly the schools. A policy of maximum openness should be pursued, including constant reporting to the parents' representatives, and through them to all the parents, about any extreme behaviors (without giving

identifying details about the children involved) and about the actions being taken to combat such phenomena. The principle of openness is closely related to the principle of territorial sovereignty, because parents will be willing to respect school territory if the school lets them in on what goes on in it. Applying the principle of openness will enable the school to receive maximum help from the parents in applying a program of nonviolent resistance. The principle of openness also guarantees the support of the parents' committee and the parents in general in dealing with the pressures of individual parents to make special allowances for children who commit disciplinary violations. Such pressures often paralyze the school in its dealing with children's violent behavior.

CASE 6: LITTLE BIG MAN

Ron was four and a half and short for his age. Despite his size, he almost caused a rebellion of parents in his kindergarten. At first, the problem looked routine: Ron had a hard time staying focused on a task, followed directions only partially, and sometimes disrupted the teacher's work. He also gave other kids hard pats on the back, uninvited caresses, and strong hugs. At the end of his first month in kindergarten, the teacher invited his mother for a conference. Both sides came out unhappy: the teacher felt the mother was unwilling to cooperate, and the mother felt the teacher did not like Ron. By then both parents had complained to the teacher's supervisor, and she promised to "set things straight." She instructed the teacher to send Ron to her office any time he got out of hand. Ron was sent to the principal a few times but his behavior did not improve. He often got out of his seat in the middle of "circle time," went over to her again and again, fondled her in the middle of her work, or started talking to her regardless of the circumstances.

The kindergarten psychologist offered the following intervention: the teacher was to tell the children that each person's regular seat during circle time was his "home." Just as you don't go into someone's home without getting permission from the owner, you do not go into someone else's "home" in kindergarten without their permission. Any child that wants to "come over" to one of their friends' houses during circle time had to get their permission. The teacher's seat, too, is her "home." Disrespect of someone's "home" would lead to the child's return to his seat without answering his questions. Ron accepted the idea of the "home" well. His visits to the teacher without permission diminished, although it was still hard for him to control his uninvited visits to the "homes" of the children sitting near him.

The "home" idea had a big impact on the other children, too. They adopted the term and even asked each other for permission to "visit." Their questions to the teacher became much more orderly. One day the teacher hurt her head in a small accident, and the children lined up requesting to "visit" her home to give her a hug.

At this time the psychologist gave a workshop about parental presence for the parents of children with discipline problems at home and in kindergarten. One of the workshop's goals was to create continuity between the kindergarten and the home. Ron's mother came to every session, but his father refused to participate.

Participation in the workshop did not dispel the mother's suspicious attitude toward the teacher. The rift between the parents and the teacher deepened because of the father's declared objection to the "time out" policy employed at the kindergarten (the children were taken by the teacher's aide to a quiet corner for five minutes each time they behaved aggressively). Once the father burst into the kindergarten and shouted at the teacher over the "time out" policy, in front of the children. After this outburst, Ron's behavior further deteriorated and he hit many children (one to the point of bleeding) and broke the teacher's aide's arm. These events led a group of parents to organize and demand that Ron be thrown out of the kindergarten. Under these circumstances, the mother and the staff became willing to employ a systematic program of nonviolent resistance to handle Ron's violence.

The program was launched with a sit-in in the kindergarten in the afternoon hours with the mother, the supervisor, the psychologist, the teacher, the aide, and Ron. The psychologist handed out a detailed instruction sheet to all the adults.

At the start of the sit-in, the mother was asked to say the following to Ron: "We are sitting here together because of your hitting the teacher, the aide and the other children in your kindergarten. We are going to sit here until you tell us what you are going to do so that there will be no more hitting." At first Ron did not respond. A long silence ensued, in which he began occupying himself in various ways: he walked around the room, crawled under the table, looked at the clock a lot, tried to open the locked door, looked at the key cabinet, and even licked one of the keys. Half an hour later he started asking his mother when they were leaving. The psychologist reminded him that he had to make a suggestion that would stop the hitting. Ron continued to roam around the room. Suddenly, he sat on the teacher's lap and hugged her. She hugged him back. A few minutes later he did it again, and got another hug. After a while the mother asked Ron: "Why do you hit?" Ron answered: "After I hit I calm down." This statement paved the way to an agreement. Ron promised to tell the teacher or the aide that he needs help before hitting. Ron also suggested that every time somebody annoyed him he would put his hands on his ears so as not to hear and not to hit. The level of violence dropped considerably in the days following the sit-in. Unfortunately, the teacher got sick a few days later, and Ron went back to his violent behavior, but recovered when the teacher called him (at the kindergarten) and reminded him of the agreement.

The sit-in bore fruit at home, too. The mother became more determined and started employing "time outs." Ron responded by asking: "Is it the same time out like in kindergarten?" She answered in the affirmative. This event created continuity between kindergarten and home, a process that was made possible particularly because the mother changed her attitude toward the teacher. The sit-in in the kindergarten showed her that her negative view of the teacher was not justified. The improved cooperation between them was significant enough to compensate for the lack of cooperation from the father. At one of the parent workshop sessions, the mother reported far-reaching changes in Ron's behavior at home. Ron's disruptions at the kindergarten almost disappeared. The teacher's presence in Ron's emotional life came through in a game at kindergarten, where the teacher invited each child to take turns playing. Ron raised his hand and began shouting: "You don't see me! You don't see me!" The teacher answered: "You are always in my heart." Ron responded with wonder: "I am in your heart, always?" The teacher nodded and Ron lowered his hand and waited patiently for his turn.

CASE 7: THE "FUN PUNISHMENT"

Nine-year-old Boris was waiting for a placement committee. The teacher wanted him transferred to special education because he was out of control. He had tantrums in class, threw chairs, threatened the teacher, and slammed tables on the floor. Intellectually, Boris was very advanced and got good grades, and he was socially popular. Boris was sent for neurological testing, but the results did not justify medical treatment. At home Boris demanded instant satisfaction of his demands. His parents knew how to maneuver, sometimes by partial submission and sometimes by diplomacy, but the teacher did not have the means or the conditions to employ such a complex strategy.

The threat of the placement committee was helpful at least in one sense: now the parents were willing to do anything to stave it off. In this situation a plan of action was developed: the mother, who worked nearby, promised to come take Boris out of school immediately every time the teacher called her. For this purpose the parents furnished the teacher with a mobile phone. The day after every event that required sending Boris home, his father was to take him with him to work. The father was instructed neither to entertain nor to punish his son, but just take him along to all the errands and all the travel required by his workday at the office. For part of the day the father had to occupy Boris with simple work-related tasks. The suggested plan made the teacher, the principal, and the parents raise their eyebrows. They viewed the time spent with the father as a sort of prize for Boris for his outbursts. The psychologist explained that the goal was neither to reward nor to punish but to increase parental presence and thereby to underscore the teacher's authority. The psychologist explained to the parents that the support they gave the teacher would strengthen her ("The teacher will become taller because she will be standing on your shoulders") and that involving the parents in school life would increase their presence ("Your field of vision grows because you can see through the teacher's eyes, too").

Over a period of six weeks, Boris spent three days with his father at work. At first he was thrilled by the "punishment," but he soon discovered the workday was long and often boring. Sometimes Boris fell asleep on a chair at work. Although the program diverged pronouncedly from any routine conception of rewards and punishments, the outbursts at school stopped completely and Boris's participation in schoolwork increased. The establishment of continuity between the parents' and teachers' positions proved highly effective in increasing the influence of both sides. The placement committee was dropped from the agenda.

CASE 8: THE SUPERVISION NETWORK

For some five months, fifteen-year-old Sean missed a lot of classes, cut entire days of school, ignored the teachers' attempts to call him to order, and responded to them provocatively. His grades, which had been good in middle school, dropped sharply. His mother responded to the teacher's attempts to involve her with a resolute defense of her son, even giving him permission slips for his absences. In a round of talks the psychologist held with the teachers, he found helplessness and rage at Sean. It turned out that two teachers had not seen him even once that year, and of those who saw him more frequently, there were some who would rather not see him.

The psychologist invited the parents to a conference, but only the mother came. She described the father as stern and disconnected and feared that if he knew what was happening, he would get violent with Sean. She described her son as a gentle and fearful boy and said he had lately become depressed and closed. She explained she had defended her son and given him false notes because she was afraid of an escalation and of an extreme reaction from Sean or the father. A year earlier her good friend's son had committed suicide, which made her deeply afraid for Sean. The psychologist voiced respect for her concern, but commented that the current situation could leave Sean in a vacuum of both parental and teacher presence. Compounded by school failures, the situation might deepen his depressed feelings. The psychologist offered to help build a supervision and protection program for Sean, which would include explicit instructions to the father on how to avoid losing control. The emphasis on working with the father to prevent outbursts and working with the teachers to create supervision without punishments gave the mother confidence, and she agreed to bring her husband in. When the father understood the program included clear resistance to Sean's school avoidance and evasiveness, he agreed to desist from using force and avoiding any hostile response toward Sean. In this way the nonviolent resistance program was a bridge between the mother and the father, and between the parents and the school.

The program that was designed was meant to show Sean involvement in his life during all school hours and an unremitting but nonviolent resistance to his patterns of avoidance and disconnection. Special attention was given to "closing the holes in the supervision network," through which Sean used to slip. The father took the responsibility of bringing Sean to the school office every morning. The secretary wrote Sean's time of arrival down on a form posted in the teachers' lounge. Throughout the day each teacher wrote on the form whether Sean came to class on time and whether he participated in it normally. Untoward behaviors were marked in a separate column. At the end of the day the homeroom teacher or the grade supervisor, who split the responsibility for this task between them over the week, examined the daily page. They gave a detailed telephone report of the day's events to the mother. In the evening both parents went into Sean's room, went over the form with him (it was faxed to them daily), and asked him how he planned to avoid repeating the negative features the next day. Every three days the teacher or the supervisor, in turns, met with Sean to summarize his progress.

Sean was very surprised by the relationship that was built between his parents and the school. He asked his mother several times what she talked about with his teacher, in a voice expressing a mixture of protest and appreciation. Sean was also surprised by his daily conversations with his parents: his father's involvement and cooperation with his mother were new experiences for him. His absences from school started to diminish just three days after the program began and stopped almost entirely within two weeks. The provocative behaviors stopped. At a summary meeting with the parents, the teacher, the supervisor, and a psychologist, the mother reported a significant change in Sean's behavior even in areas the program did not touch, and the father enthusiastically added his observations. Sean's grades rose steeply, and at the end of the year he received a personal letter from the principal expressing appreciation for his successful effort. The following year the formal supervision was lifted, without any noticeable harm to his functioning. The father, whose daily drives to school with Sean became meaningful to him, continued bringing Sean to school.

8 NONVIOLENT RESISTANCE IN THE COMMUNITY

In the preceding chapters we discussed transferring nonviolent resistance, originally developed to fight oppression and violence on the socio-political level, to the family sphere. In this chapter we return to the social dimension and examine the implications of nonviolent resistance for therapeutic and prevention programs in the community. The issues in this chapter pertain not to individuals, but rather to negative norms, which have been adopted or are in danger of being adopted by large groups. These norms include activities such as young people's alcohol and drug parties, driving all-terrain vehicles (ATVs) without a license, boycotts and violence against individuals and groups, and night loitering for shady purposes. In this chapter we examine some of the opportunities nonviolent resistance offers to deal with these negative practices.

THE FEATURES OF NONVIOLENT RESISTANCE IN THE COMMUNITY

Nonviolent resistance in community settings is characterized by the readiness of the activists to cross boundaries that were previously viewed as sacrosanct and by activists' continuous efforts to build alliances.

Crossing Boundaries

To implement nonviolent resistance, parents, educators, and other community agents must evolve a readiness to cross the "red lines"

171

that govern expectations and conventions between adults and teens. Nonviolent resistance activists have to enter places that are considered taboo for them. From this point of view, every act of nonviolent resistance contains an element of social scandal, of something that is not done, and which contradicts previously inviolable tacit agreements. Still, the "scandals" of nonviolent resistance are clearly distinguishable from other intentional scandalous acts, for these usually involve an active provocation, whereas the acts of nonviolent resistance strictly avoid any provocative or inflammatory gestures.

Gandhi was the great master of the paradoxical art of creating "scandals through restraint." Gandhi informed the British High Commissioner in India of his intention to implement nonviolent resistance against the British salt monopoly. With this public declaration, Gandhi violated two conventions: one, obeying the law, and the other, that violations of the law should be done in secret. Gandhi announced that he was embarking on a journey to the sea by a route he publicized in advance, to personally mine salt. If the British wanted to arrest him, Gandhi added, he would not resist, but his followers would continue the journey en masse, would reach the sea, and would mine salt. The activists were carefully instructed to avoid being drawn into provocations, even if they were physically assaulted. The legions of activists, who crowded the beaches and exposed their bodies to the policemen's beatings without trying to defend themselves, were an incredible sight. Their restraint greatly increased the scandal of the prohibited salt mining. On reaching the sea, Gandhi mined salt with his own hands. This act of overt civil disobedience was undertaken without any impassioned declarations: flags were not burned and chants against the occupiers were not voiced. The physical presence at the beach, the hand reaching into the water, and the scooping out of the first handful of salt are emblematic acts of how nonviolent resistance is embodied by the quiet personal presence of the resister. This act expresses the message: "I am here, the beach is ours, we cannot be prevented from reaching it, nor can millions be prevented from reaching it and mining salt." The strength that the activists drew from that act and the power of the protest were in direct proportion to the legal and conventional boundaries that were crossed and to the activists' ability to withstand all provocations to violence.

The need to shatter conventions that lies at the basis of nonviolent resistance explains the inhibition that prevents many adults from taking the necessary steps. In the following examples, we underline the power of the tacit taboo that forbids many adults from entering areas we call the "realm of youth." Adults' inhibitions and hesitations do not mean they are unmotivated. Their inhibitions can be overcome with information and support. The hidden taboo should be pointed out, and the need to shatter it made clear. Even then, however, the activists cannot be expected to undertake the daring necessary steps alone. For this reason, the forces of resistance must be consolidated and public support be obtained. This will enable the responsible adults in the community to shatter the paralyzing conventions and resist the teens' destructive actions even at the heart of their territory.

We must remember that the very willingness to turn to external parties for help is in itself the breach of a taboo – the taboo of preserving discretion and privacy, which often paralyzes not only parents, but also the actions of educators and other community agents. Overcoming the self-imposed imperative of maintaining discretion at all costs can have a decisive impact on the community struggle against violence. For instance, the prevailing expectation that the school resolve problems that come up inside it without involving external parties weakens and paralyzes it. On the other hand, the decision to expose such problems and turn to others for help (especially when the decision is made out of free will and is not imposed from the outside in the wake of unexpected exposure of violent episodes) strengthens the positive forces inside and outside the school.

Building Alliances

Just as in the family, in the community, too, it is vital to break out of isolation and build alliances with parties who support the fight against violence and self-destructiveness. Such alliances strengthen the resolve to act, increase the authority and legitimacy of the measures taken, and lead to an increasing isolation of the voices that favor the negative options. Just as in the family, such alliances may help to mobilize the dormant or hidden positive voices within the "realm of youth."

To encourage these voices, the appropriate conditions have to be provided. For this purpose, the "us-them" polarity (e.g., adults-children or teachers-students) has to be overcome. This polarization makes it easier for the violent or otherwise antisocial youths to exercise pressure on those that wish to oppose these trends. Various means can be deployed to reduce the polarization: reconciliation gestures, use of mediators, restrained language, creating mixed groups of youths and adults who oppose violence, and so on. Actions that reduce polarization are therefore crucial for the success of nonviolent resistance on the community level.

A COMMUNITY PROJECT: ATVS AND ALCOHOL PARTIES

The initiative for the following community project came from an Israeli regional high school that had students from five villages spread over a thirty-kilometer radius. The goal of the project was defined as "restoring the authority of adults in the community" (Kenigswald 2001). The project involved the teachers and other members of the school administration, parent committees, and a number of communal bodies.

Two negative norms had taken root among the youngsters of the community: driving ATVs without licenses and holding alcohol parties. The alcohol parties became normative from grade nine and up, and among the ATV drivers were children as young as twelve. Sometimes the kids drove the ATVs a long distance to their alcohol parties, after which they raced home drunk in the middle of the night. Attempts by a community police officer to write up the violating children, in order to send a report to the legal authorities, were blocked by a group of fathers. The fathers demanded that the head of the regional council explain to the strict police officer that different rules applied to their frontier region than to the big cities. This argument was characterized by other parents, who opposed the norm but felt helpless to change it, as reflecting a "Wild West mentality." The parents who favored looser regulations opined that their children were missing many of the pleasures open to youth in the vibrant urban centers, and that they should therefore be compensated for their loss. The dangerous norm was thus upheld by this desire of a minority to provide their children with the freedom of the wilderness. The pressure applied by the small group of permissive fathers bore fruit: the police officer stopped attending to ATV drivers and limited himself to writing traffic reports for cars that drove by on the main highway. Everyone knew that a parent who dared protest against the norm would quickly become unpopular with the kids. But most of the parents were very afraid. Two ATVs had overturned shortly before the project began, and the writing was on the wall.

After a lecture at school to all the parents about the principles of parental presence and nonviolent resistance, a campaign against the ATVs was launched. It was coordinated by a community worker who made sure to receive support and backing from the parents as a group. Only after the program was approved by vote of a large majority of parents in each of the villages were any practical measures taken. A letter signed by the parent representatives was sent to the council head and the community police officer, and a copy was distributed to all the parents. The letter said that the parents had a list of thirty children who drove without licenses, and that they demanded this be stopped immediately. The parents of the children in question were warned by the parent representatives that if the violation recurred, they would act resolutely to take legal measures against them. In this state of affairs it became clear to the "Wild West" people that the council head could no longer be pressured into ignoring the phenomenon. The act of parental resistance was accompanied by a reconciliation gesture: a course in ATV driving was offered gratis by the local council to children who had reached the appropriate age of seventeen, which in Israel is the legal age for obtaining a driver's license (for ATVs as well as for regular cars); the children who took this course and passed the test then became legitimate drivers. Inviting these older children to the course brought them over to the legal side, thus reducing the "us-them" polarity between children and adults. As a result of this process, the other children and their parents had to accept the reality. This combination of resolve and reconciliation achieved its goal: the parents who had previously supported the lawless behavior restrained their children, and the driving without licenses stopped. Two of the "Wild West" fathers even changed their stripes and claimed it was they who had "tied the horse."

The success strengthened the activists' belief that the second goal could be achieved: preventing alcohol parties. The first step was to pass a resolution that all public buildings would be closed to parties that included the use of alcohol. This led to a diminution in the size of the alcohol parties, which from now on had to be conducted in private homes. Now the parents faced the harder task: to intervene in the alcohol parties taking place in private homes.

At a meeting of parents of ninth graders, some expressed their willingness to intervene. Five parents wanted to act immediately: they went into a party that was in full swing, collected the bottles that were on the table, and announced to the kids they would come again to check whether alcohol was being consumed. The intervention broke up the party. The kids dispersed and some started complaining about the "tattletales," among whom were named the children of two of the parents who had busted the party, although they had nothing to do with the parents' action. It was clear that in order to continue with the intervention, the support of additional parents was needed, to take turns supervising parties and to prevent this measure from being identified with the parents of certain children. This is where a difficulty came up: of some twenty parents who had come to another meeting at the school and who had expressed their support for the program, only five ultimately went into classrooms to inform the kids of the joint decision to make regular visits to their parties. The other parents, the community worker was later told, "got cold feet." The expression sounds strange, since the parents did not face any danger of a severe reaction by the children. It can be understood, however, as a result of the inhibition that parents felt about breaking the privacy taboo by invading a private party. The end of the intervention was disappointing. A youth counselor who refused to put up with the initiative's waning went into a party herself and confiscated the bottles. This action drew a series of telephone calls in which she was cursed and threatened. She complained about it to the parents' representatives, but their support flagged. Due to the lack of backing, the counselor decided to resign from her job and move away from the area.

The parental inhibition in this case points to a more general taboo against crossing the boundary into the "realm of youth." There are few adults who do not feel a strong reluctance against showing up in places such as dance clubs, youth parties, video stores, or street corners that are regular meeting places for teenagers. Entering these places would be viewed as a particularly grave infringement if done at times that are viewed as the exclusive preserve of the "realm of youth," namely, the night time, weekends, and holidays. Children, for their part, will apply heavy pressure on their friends to not tell adults about things that they view as belonging to their realm. Such sharing would be defined as "tattletaling" and would expose the informer to severe acts of retribution. The parents' failure to enter the alcohol parties is an example of automatic respect for this taboo. The parental avoidance of action is tantamount to a spontaneous act of self-censorship and voluntary acceptance of the prohibitions. As we see below, the success of nonviolent resistance often hinges on persuading the adults to cross the boundaries and break the taboos. The following community initiative that originated in the Netherlands illustrates this willingness.

THE "NEIGHBORHOOD FATHERS"

The locus of this community action was a crime-infested immigrant neighborhood in Amsterdam that had already witnessed massive street battles between young immigrants and the police. The initiative by seven members of the neighborhood to establish a civil guard to prevent youth violence on the streets was met with resistance from various parties. The police, to whom the volunteers went to receive help (raincoats, walkie-talkies, photocopying facilities) were reserved about the idea: how could inexperienced and untrained people succeed where weathered police forces had failed? The kids on the street suspected the idea was a police plot to recruit informers from the neighborhood. The volunteers' wives also tried to dissuade them, fearing for their safety. In spite of their differences, the forces that opposed the project shared a common assumption: everyone knows that at night the streets belong to the young people. The wish of the project initiators to contest these widely accepted territorial rights constituted a severe breach of the tacit agreement between grownups and youth. The seven parents (later nicknamed the "neighborhood fathers") were not deterred. They started nightly patrols from 9 P.M. to 1 A.M. They distributed leaflets to the homes stating that members of the guard would address the kids any time they thought disturbances were emerging and would ask them to disperse. If necessary, members of the guard would contact the kids' parents and ask them to come. Children under the age of fourteen found on the street unaccompanied or without a reasonable explanation would be accompanied home by members of the guard. Alternatively, the volunteers would call their parents and ask them to come get them.

Resistance to the idea quickly waned. In two months the number of volunteers reached twenty-three and the violent incidents in the quarter dropped by more than half. The members of the guard got to know the boys and their families. Some of the families embraced the project and provided the volunteers with food and services. At this stage it became clear the kids were not all of one cloth, and some began cooperating, for instance, by helping the "fathers" to persuade the others to disperse. The police, too, changed their position and provided the volunteers with marking tape, a gathering station, radios, and frequencies. An important turning point for the police and the public was the success of the "fathers" in calming passions stirred by a soccer game between Morocco and the Netherlands. The success led to the project being replicated in other quarters and cities.

The story is particularly surprising because the measures applied were so simple: the presence of adults in the "realm of youth" and the growing support of the neighborhood's residents, some of the young people, and finally the police, too. The readiness to cross boundaries and the establishment of alliances led to success in a task that was hitherto viewed as impracticable.

NONVIOLENT RESISTANCE IN SCHOOLS

Most successful programs against violence and vandalism in schools share the same two principles: (1) crossing boundaries and establishing adult presence in violence-prone areas, and (2) establishing alliances in the community at large and with the children in particular (Goldstein 1996; Goldstein & Conoley 1997; Mayer et al. 1983; Olweus 1993; Smith et al. 1999). It is interesting to note that in most of the programs these principles were applied on a pragmatic basis without a clear conceptual basis. Nonviolent resistance is the first approach to put these two elements at the center. Here we see how the systematic use of these principles and of the basic concepts of nonviolent resistance may help us avoid mistakes and improve the effectiveness of interventions.

Polarizing Mistakes

Here is a familiar scenario: on hearing about acts of violence or bullying in a certain classroom or grade, the principal stands before the children, makes a strong speech against violence, and threatens severe punishments. The desired deterrence is usually not achieved, and often the results are the opposite. Not only do the victims not receive protection, they may even be subject to an additional dose of violence because of their presumed "tattletaling." The failure is due to the blatant violation of the principles of nonviolent resistance: (1) the principal's threatening appearance increases the polarization between the adult camp and the children's camp; (2) the principal's tone conveys the message "I am the boss," encouraging the aggressive children to try to prove otherwise; (3) the principal is acting alone, without first mobilizing the community or the children; and (4) the threat increases the siege within the "realm of youth" on the potential informers. None of these elements bodes well for the victims or the other children.

For a deeper understanding of the processes that doom such interventions to failure, we must look at what happens inside the children's camp. The "realm of youth" tends to develop its own division of power, as well as mechanisms of judgment and punishment. These often become manifest in group boycotts or harassment of defenseless children, in the growth of overpowering cliques, and in battles for dominance among competing groups. We would venture that the less contact there is between the adults and the children, the greater will be the cruelty of these processes within the "realm of youth." On occasion, the punishing measures assume awful proportions, and anyone suspected of breaking rank is in particular danger. The reigning principle is: "This is our territory, and anyone who turns it over to the grown-ups or cooperates with them is a traitor!" "Tattletaling" is thus the worst crime in this value system. The child who turns to adults for help proves himself a worthless coward and merits extreme punishment for disclosing the children's world to alien eyes.

One of the damages wrought by the principal's threatening speech is that it deepens and strengthens these processes. Studies of group violence (bullying and boycotts) toward weak individuals or groups showed that the vast majority (some 85 percent) of violent incidents in school take place in full view of groups of uninvolved children (Craig & Pepler 1997). The bullies and their helpers, just like the victims, comprise a small minority of the children, while the uninvolved children are the vast majority (Salmivalli 1999; Salmivalli et al. 1996). This majority silently sides with the victims (Rigby & See 1992), but under normal conditions prefers not to intervene or turn to the adults (Craig & Pepler 1997). These tendencies intensify, the greater the polarization between adults and children: it is the well-known phenomenon of closing ranks, which we have seen in parents or teachers who feel accused and threatened. The principal's threatening appearance can be expected to lead the children to close ranks, much reducing the chances that the noninvolved children will take an active stance against the violent ones. Nonviolent resistance strives for the opposite outcome: reducing the polarization and building bridges to the silent majority, hoping to dissuade them from their stance of nonintervention and to mobilize them to resist the violence.

In many programs designed to combat vandalism, we witness the same polarizing actions on the part of adults. For instance, an approach to violence and vandalism that has become popular in the United States in the last decade is based on fortifying the physical environment and the objects prone to vandalistic attack. Schools that take this approach introduce physical barriers, such as fortified glass, anti-graffiti paint, massive tables, benches, and chairs, hermetic closure and fencing off of the school, planting of shrubbery to prevent passage, placing of signs and decorative elements beyond reach, identification of students by personal cards, smoke detectors, alarm systems, and closed circuit television (Clarke 1992; Wood 1991). Not only are these means extremely expensive, they also give up in advance all chances to change the vandalistic tendencies or the silent majority's inclination not to intervene. Most likely, the use of fortifications as an answer to vandalism deepens the tendency not to intervene, by conveying the message: "We adults are in charge of preservation, while you children are in charge of destruction!" There is no doubt that the atmosphere in a school where defense measures are the most prominent feature of the landscape will be alienating and polarized. Critics of this approach have said that the existence of fortifications on such a scale actually presents a constant challenge for the vandal's inventiveness.

Mobilizing Support and Creating a Larger "We" Against Violence

The mobilization of support in the struggle against violence and vandalism is the key to a persuasive show of presence and a successful bridging between the adult and youth camps. Among the groups worth recruiting are student and parent representatives and community agents and officials (e.g., social workers, probation officers, or police officers). A group that deserves special attention is young adults who are not yet identified by the children with the adult world: these people can serve a key function in serving as a bridge between the camps. For instance, in an intervention we conducted in two community high schools we obtained the support of former students who had recently graduated from the school. The importance of including them was that these people are not seen by the children as clearly belonging with the school authorities or the adult world. They form rather an intermediate level that makes it easier for most of the kids to cooperate. The support of this intermediate group reduces the stigma of "treason" that hinders many kids from addressing the school authorities directly when they witness events of violence against other children. Mobilizing these different groups serves to bolster the ranks of all those who would like to oppose the violence. The message now is: "We are not alone!" and "We will no longer keep the violence secret!"

Including the police in a program of nonviolent resistance may raise eyebrows, but it may have considerable advantages. (1) Including the police in the program may promote their positive involvement and prevent untoward consequences. Our experience in working with families of violent children showed that involving the police as part of the therapeutic program allowed for more productive, controlled, and reversible interventions (e.g., the chances of stopping legal procedures in the case of improvement are better). On the other hand, going to the police in an acute situation, without prior contact, can lead to serious consequences for both the children and the parents. In schools, too, the early inclusion of the police leads to dialogue and maximum effectiveness, while including them out of necessity in an acute situation can have more unpredictable results. (2) Inviting the police conveys a message of determination to fight the violence, whereas the systematic avoidance of this option may convey the contrary message. (3) Including the police makes it possible to deal with elements from outside the school that incite the violence inside it.

Recruiting supporters takes time, but their response is usually very favorable and the positive effects are quickly noticeable. This is particularly true when they are approached in the name of a program of nonviolent resistance. The high moral standing of nonviolent resistance is obvious to all, and leads potential supporters to identify rapidly with it.

Including members of the various support groups can have a decisive effect on the students' involvement in the nonviolent resistance program. Now the students are no longer addressed by an authority figure using threatening language that deepens polarization ("Watch out!" "I warn you!"). Instead, the students are positively appealed to together with the members of other support groups. The use of "we" to include everyone, adults and children, who wishes to oppose the rule of violence cannot but have a deep mobilizing effect.

Under these conditions one can only wonder why school officials usually avoid mobilizing external help. Schools, like families, no doubt view public exposure as threatening. However, just as in families, the decision to keep violence secret perpetuates it. Another reason for neglecting external support may be that the school authorities still hope that adequate deterrence can be achieved by using the strict, traditional disciplinary means. This belief usually turns out to be naïve.

The program of nonviolent resistance may be launched with an opening event that involves all the potential supporters inside and outside the school. After the goals of the program are defined, the representatives of the various mobilized groups may introduce themselves to the students and state their interest and potential contribution in the fight against violence. After the opening event, there should be discussions in the various classrooms. Several of the external representatives should enter each class. Dividing the forum into the classes will allow the students more freedom to raise problems and offer solutions. Thereby the students can be mobilized not only as passive clients, but also as active partners in the fight against violence. The class discussion has the following goals.

1. To allow as many students as possible to express themselves about the violence.

2. To have a practical discussion of avenues to increase reporting of violent incidents (such as a "hotline" from representatives of the student council or a box of anonymous complaints), ways to address existing weaknesses in the protection of students (such as mapping out the locations where the increased presence of adults is needed), and suggestions to repair equipment damaged as a result of vandalism.

3. To have a critical discussion of the question of "tattletaling," with the goal of challenging the common assumption that reporting violence is an instance of denunciatory behavior. For example, one could point to the difference between a report of a student copying in a test (which would count as "tattletaling") and a report aimed at saving a friend who is the victim of assault, blackmail, or boycott. The role played in this discussion by school graduates may be crucial, for their presentation of the desired position cannot be discounted by their being identified with the adult world. In the community schools where we included such young graduates in the discussion, these were the people who successfully defended the supreme value of not abandoning a friend in danger. These discussions also exposed the hypocritical use by the bullies of the concept of "tattletaling," when their only goal is to maintain their rule.

These discussions offer the students the possibility of defining themselves as members of the larger community of people involved in the fight against violence and vandalism. Creating this new and broader "we" overshadows the previous strict division between the adults' and the children's camps. Research has shown that creating such a supercommunity is key to the success of programs to combat vandalism.

One such successful program was carried out in the 1980s in quarters of various Israeli cities with high crime rates. The project was organized by the national police and was based on the creation of

groups of "property trustees." These were made out of teens, organized in patrols, who showed presence in school territory during the
times when most cases of vandalism occurred (mainly weekends and
holidays). The goal of the project was not only to reduce the scope of
damage to property, but also to bring the youngsters closer in a positive way to the law-enforcing agencies. For instance, in a project in
the town of Ramleh in the summer of 1990, some 800 children were
recruited from a number of schools. The participants received special
hats and sleeve tags. Their role was to patrol the schools' entrances
and yards on weekends and during the summer holidays. Compared
with twelve serious incidents of break-in and sabotage during the
same period in the previous year, there was not a single such episode
during the period of the project (Geva 1992). During that time, the
involvement of youth in other kinds of criminal activity dropped
sharply.

The research literature reports several projects that have demonstrated similar effectiveness. For instance, students from a slum in
an American city went on patrols in the community and recruited
supporters to fight vandalism and improve the school's appearance.
The goal was to bring the children closer to various community bodies. The teachers, too, were included in organizing the patrols and
creating contacts with the community bodies. The program led to
a substantial drop in the level of vandalism over the years. The organizers conducted an accurate calculation of the money saved by
the project: in one school the savings reached 92 percent of the annual expenditure on repairs (Mayer et al. 1983). Some of the money
that was saved was channeled to covering the costs of recreational
activities for the students.

The idea of creating motivation through the use of the money
saved and of thus establishing a new "we" identity of the students
opposing vandalism proved itself in Israel, too. The principal of a
middle school in a small Israeli town asked the head of the local
council to support her struggle against vandalism by investing "venture capital" at the rate of half the annual expenses on repairing
school property. On hearing the details of her plan, he agreed. At

the beginning of the school year, the principal told the students that each class had a specified sum of money for repairs of their class's equipment for the whole year. Classes that managed to keep at least 90 percent of the original sum in their coffers would be rewarded by having that sum doubled. To everyone's surprise, all but one class managed to meet the 90 percent requirement. Representatives of the class that failed went to the principal and asked to do volunteer repairs in order to reach the sum that would win them the bonus. The principal agreed, and this class, too, after whitewashing the school, received the bonus. Part of the success in these cases was probably due to the successful overshadowing, by the emergent "we" identity of all those interested in fighting vandalism, of the traditional "us-them" polarity that often sets up a chasm between children and adults. The vandalistic act ceased to be an expression of students' angry protest against the school authorities and was now perceived as an act that harmed the class's common interest. Instead of the child who resisted vandalism being stigmatized as a "tattletale," now the vandals themselves became the "traitors" who harmed the common interest.

The Presence of Adults in Violence-Prone Areas

The act of nonviolent resistance crosses the hidden boundaries that define the territories "belonging" to the children. Research on violence in schools shows that most violent incidents occur in a small number of places. The salient characteristic of those places is that they are "adult free." Unfortunately, these territories do not belong equally to all of the children but belong only to the minority among them who are willing to use force and intimidation to stake their claim of ownership. The reestablishment of adult presence in those areas leads to a substantial drop in violence (Olweus 1993; Smith et al. 1999). Physical presence, as we saw in the chapters about families, is what conveys the clearest message of resistance to violence.

The teachers are often saddled with the task of reestablishing physical presence in these areas. However, attempts to activate the teachers without prior persuasion and in the absence of support or involvement of additional parties are doomed to fail. Teachers do not feel they were trained to deal with violence or that it is their job. The expectation that they serve as guards in the hallways, yards, school entrances, and students' bathrooms infuriates and scares them. Laying the responsibility on the teachers, often while threatening them and attacking their "elusiveness" or "laziness," makes matters worse.

Teachers in this situation are in a position similar to that of parents dealing with aggressive and violent children in the family. As in the family, teachers cannot be expected to muster their courage and heroically show up in the problematic areas. Only when they feel they are no longer isolated nor blamed but receive the appropriate support will they become able and willing to join a demanding nonviolent resistance program. As we showed in the previous chapter, the habit of blaming teachers and placing categorical demands on them heightens their loneliness and weakens their authority. To involve them successfully, wider support needs to be created and logistical networks need to be built. These networks differ depending on the situation and the institution. Thus the presence of teachers in problem areas has been variously bolstered by other adults, such as volunteers from the community, parents, or paid guards. In the face of such a broad mobilization, the teachers will not stand aside, and their contribution to increasing adult presence can be very significant.

Teachers' willingness to undertake such a project is grounded in their understanding that increasing their presence beyond the classroom serves their professional, public, and personal interests. Teachers understand well that their status is badly hurt by confining their influence to the classroom. Turning the areas outside the classroom into the exclusive preserve of the "realm of youth" necessarily has negative effects on conducting the classes. Kids wandering through the hallways, going out in the middle of classes, and coming into classes late are all the result of the hallways and the yards being "adult free" areas. Moreover, the various kinds of violence (bullying, boycotts, group harassment, and gang competition) do not cease the moment the students enter the classroom. Thus the rule of the aggressive children infiltrates the area under the formal jurisdiction of the teacher. These processes turn the unsupported teacher, whose influence has been narrowed to the confines of the classroom, into a besieged person. The result often is the rapid burnout of the teacher. A teacher who understands this will not refuse an offer to restore her status by increasing her presence if the offer is based on an understanding of her predicament and will enable her to break out of her loneliness. In schools where we offered the teaching staff programs in the spirit of nonviolent resistance, the teachers showed an impressive willingness to buckle down to the task. We have no doubt that just like a parent whose authority has been eroded, so, too, a teacher would choose to break out of her passivity and confinement if she had the appropriate support. The argument that teachers will not cooperate because they do not want to be bothered is baseless slander that reflects the fashionable hostility against teachers.

A Modified Suspension Procedure

The measures described above will lead to a reduction of violent episodes, to a narrowing of "blind spots," and to an increased willingness of teachers and students to become involved in the struggle against violence. But they do not provide an answer to the violent incidents that will occur despite declaring the fight, mobilizing the support, reducing the polarization, and increasing adult presence. In other words, all the recruitment and prevention measures are no substitute for sanctions. The following suggestion is an attempt to redesign the common sanction of suspension in the spirit of nonviolent resistance. The goal is to turn this weatherworn sanction into a tool to strengthen the message conveyed by the entire nonviolent resistance program.

It is no secret that suspension in its usual form has little effectiveness. There are a few reasons.

1. Suspension removes the child from the school atmosphere and undermines his feeling of belonging to it, and thereby increases the polarization.

2. Usually parents are the passive party in the suspension process and object to its use. This often leads to their increased alienation from the school.

3. Aggressive children feel the need to present their suspension terms as "holidays" where they do whatever they please, which is often close to the truth.

4. The usual suspension process has no means to promote the reintegration of the child in the class and school.

All of the above make suspensions a very problematic sanction. Nonetheless, schools are wary of giving up this sanction for serious disciplinary incidents, and asking them to avoid using it is unrealistic. In the absence of an appropriate alternative, canceling suspensions would render the school even more powerless to handle violent children. But we think the old sanction can undergo a facelift.

1. *Making violent incidents and their sanctions public.* A nonviolent resistance struggle cannot be waged while maintaining institutional discretion. As we have seen, keeping the secret perpetuates violence in the family. The situation in school is similar: attempts to preserve secrecy and to avoid exposing the violent incidents conveys the message of accepting them and prevents mobilizing support. Anyone who tries to show consideration for the violent child by keeping his actions secret must remember they are thereby abandoning the victims. The school must dare to break the taboo that prevents making violent events public.

We suggest that schools announce in advance to all the parents and the students that the fight against violence will from now on be the top priority and that the school will make every violent event public. Moreover, the school will suspend any child who is involved in a violent episode. The school will not publicize the names of those involved in the events, but naturally their identities will be an open secret to members of their class. This policy will be stressed not only in the declaration that opens the campaign, but also in every contact between the school and the parents. The justification for taking these unequivocal measures will be the same as the parents' justification of their decision to introduce third parties to their previously guarded family secret: that they will no longer put up with violence in any form. Creating such a policy and integrating it into the school rules will inoculate it against pressures to go easy in special cases.

2. *Coordinating the suspension with the parents.* It is a common mistake to inform parents of their child's suspension by letter, and they cannot but be offended by the anonymous report. In this situation, the parents often identify with the child and join him in blaming the school. This attitude leads to the desire to compensate him for the injustice done to him. The results can be grave: the parents' alienation and their mobilization alongside their law-violating child against the school. To head off this danger, the parents should be addressed directly before the suspension goes into effect. If necessary, the suspension should be delayed until they are contacted.

The talk with the parents has several goals: (1) to describe the event to the parents, (2) to remind them that suspension is the fixed school policy in any case of violence, and (3) to gain the parents' cooperation in maintaining the child's contact with the school during the period of suspension. For this purpose, school representatives should stay in touch with the child during the suspension to keep him abreast of news, to give him homework, and to encourage his successful return when his punishment ends. Sharing information with the parents about scholastic assignments during the suspension may also contribute to the measure's success.

Preventing disconnection and polarization is the paramount goal in this improved suspension model. The suspended child must continue feeling like a student of the school. In addition, the child and the parents must feel the school is cooperating with them in the search for ways to prevent the problem's recurrence. Both goals require bridging and mediating.

Scholastic assignments can be brought home to the suspended child by his classmates. It is better to send a different classmate each time, or a small committee, so that the child may experience the visits as an official event of sorts. It is also important to back up the students' visits with a phone call by the homeroom teacher to the child and parents. In this phone call, the teacher or school counselor will consult with them regarding finding an appropriate mediator who will come to discuss with the child ways to prevent future outbursts. The mediator must be someone the child trusts who is willing to visit him and raise the question of how he is going to avoid a similar embroilment in the future. The mediator can be someone from school, a counselor, a relative, or a friend who agrees to assume this task. The school will contact the mediator, describe the event to him, and ask him to visit the child and discuss the problem with him. The importance of this conversation is not only in raising practical suggestions for a solution but in the very fact of having it. The fact that a person the child accepts is trying to help him find a way to prevent the recurrence of the violence increases the school's presence in the child's life, reduces polarization, and strengthens the nonviolent resistance. The mediator must understand that even if the child does not suggest a solution, the very visit and presentation of the problem are important contributions. The mediator must be prepared for the possibility of the child spurning his mediation efforts and sticking to his hostile position. In this case, the mediator must not be drawn into an argument with the child. He must make do with a statement that if the child would like to think of a solution in the future, he will be at his disposal. In this case, the meeting may be ended by saying: "We have not found a solution yet!" This should be a statement of a fact, not a warning or a threat.

Before the child returns to school, he and his parents must be contacted to find out whether they need any help in easing his return. They should be thanked for their cooperation and offered continued contact in the weeks following the suspension. The school's willingness (represented by the teacher or the school counselor) to stay in touch with the parents even after the end of the suspension improves the chances of preventing a breakdown and promoting the success of the process. Moreover, just like a child who behaved violently at home, so, too, the child who was suspended is entitled on his return to feel fully accepted. He and his classmates should be shown that he is part of the class for every purpose.

The aforementioned measures are meant to infuse the suspension process with the principles of nonviolent resistance. Making the event public shows those involved that the school will no longer cooperate with attempts to conceal violence. The advance announcement that any violent event will lead to suspension conveys a message of nontolerance of violence. The coordination with the parents, the use of mediators, and the maintenance of contact throughout the suspension prevent the polarization that often leads to further escalation. These actions require a willingness to cross boundaries and build bridges. These are, as we know, the heart and soul of nonviolent resistance in the community.

Many of the difficulties in implementing the present suspension model can be solved by means of a standing protocol that details all the steps in the procedure. Considering that this may be the most important sanction a school can use, and that many dangers can result from its misuse, we think that writing such a protocol and abiding by it strictly are the duty of every school. We think suspension should be treated as a powerful intervention tool that requires strict rules for its use and control. Using suspension without such rules can lead to a serious breach in the relationship between parents and teachers and between school and students. On the other hand, building and introducing a suspension protocol in the spirit of nonviolent resistance will help create a safe environment at school and help underscore the parent-teacher alliance, as well as the parents' and teachers' authority.

AFTERWORD

Nonviolent Resistance as a Moral and Practical Doctrine for the Individual, the Family, and the Community

One of the reasons for the weakening of the family and the community in the modern world and the strengthening of destructive and violent patterns in children is the absence of accepted norms that provide a clear and united stance. Society, therapists, families, and even individuals within themselves move between conflicting moral poles toward the aggressive and violent child. This polarization paralyzes the adults' authority. The conflicting values typically represent opposite extremes, such as the "soft way" versus the "tough way," "making demands" versus "acceptance," "permissiveness" versus "authoritarianism," or "discipline" versus "therapy." We think much of the potential of nonviolent resistance comes from its ability to bridge these extremes. This makes nonviolent resistance morally and practically acceptable to the vast majority of parents, teachers, and therapists in our divided society.

Nonviolent resistance enables parents who are conflicted over their child-rearing attitudes to cooperate with each other, not by offering them a lukewarm compromise between the "tough" and the "soft" approaches but by a real synthesis that reinforces both. With nonviolent resistance, the "tough" parent may set limits without falling into an escalating spiral, while the "soft" one may conciliate without submitting. Moreover, the "tough" parent gets an opportunity to conciliate, and the "soft" one receives tools to protect himself and his other children against violence. In this way, the opposing approaches merge and enrich each other.

Nonviolent resistance plays a similar unifying role between parents and teachers. The common polarization between the two stems from the same conflicts that beset the "tough" and the "soft" parents. Thus the parents of the aggressive child are often cast in the role of her advocates, while the school gets the role of the prosecution. Likewise, the different community agencies often break into opposing camps. For instance, the Society for the Protection of Children would strive to protect the child's privacy, while the Authority for the War against Drugs would strive for increased supervision. Here, too, nonviolent resistance allows for bridging and for common goals. Teachers and parents unifying under the umbrella of nonviolent resistance learn to avoid the mutual neutralization, escalation, and erosion of authority that evolve out of their mutual attacks. The same is true for the different community agencies: programs based on nonviolent resistance often manage to unite parents, relatives, friends, teachers, truancy officers, social workers, probation officers, and sometimes also the child's personal therapist.

At the individual level, nonviolent resistance enables the parent to unite the conflicting internal voices competing for his attention. A parent who is afraid, for instance, that any demands on his part might detract from his empathy and acceptance, that attempting to set a limit would alienate the child, or that a firm position against violence might lead to the child's mental breakdown will learn through the practice of nonviolent resistance that behaviors that convey the message "I am your parent! I will not give up on you or give in to you!" are the optimal expression of both limits and closeness. In this way the parent curbs the violence and expresses her devotion through the very same acts.

Nonviolent resistance achieves this by being not only a moral, but also a practical doctrine. Gandhi was not only a spiritual leader, but also a great strategist. He had the amazing talent of defining such practical means and solutions that each and every one of them embodied the entire doctrine. With Gandhi, each practical measure had to withstand the most stringent moral test: to prove itself a faithful bearer of the spirit of nonviolent resistance. We tried to make this our

goal, too, in the writing of this book. We tried to offer parents, teachers, and members of the community specific and practical measures,
each of which would manifest the spirit of nonviolent resistance.
We hope this spirit is faithfully reflected in actions such as sit-ins,
telephone rounds, sit-down strikes, involving external parties, turning to public opinion, using mediators, and effecting reconciliation
measures.

It is not enough for us to demonstrate the program's effectiveness
in reducing the problematic behaviors of the child. We demand more
from it: that it show also a commensurate reduction in the parents'
outbursts and hostility levels. Our data and experience with over
400 families clearly indicate that the approach abides by these cri-
teria. But we think there is even more potential. If what we have
constructed is indeed a faithful translation of Gandhi's doctrine, we
can hope that parents, educators, community workers, therapists,
and ultimately many children, too, will be able to say not only "It
works!" but also "It is morally right!"

REFERENCES

Adler, N. A., & Schutz, J. (1995). Sibling incest offenders. *Child Abuse and Neglect, 19*, 811–819.

Alon, N., & Omer, H. (in press). The demonic and tragic narratives in psychotherapy and personal relations.

Alpert, J. (1991). Sibling, cousin, and peer child sexual abuse: Clinical implications. Paper presented at the 99th Annual Convention of the American Psychological Association, San Francisco, Calif.

Bank, S., & Kahn, M. (1982). *The sibling bond.* New York: Basic.

Bass, E., & Davis, L. (1988). *The courage to heal: A guide for women survivors of child sexual abuse.* New York: Harper & Row.

Bates, J. E., Petit, G. S., Dodge, K. A., & Ridge, B. (1998). Interaction of temperamental resistance to control and restrictive parenting in the development of externalizing behavior. *Developmental Psychology, 34*, 982–995.

Baumrind, D. (1971). Current patterns of parental authority. *Developmental Psychology Monographs, 4* (1, Pt. 2).

Baumrind, D. (1991). Effective parenting during the early adolescent transition. In P. A. Cowan & E. M. Hetherington (eds.), *Family transitions* (pp. 111–163). Hillsdale, N.J.: Lawrence Erlbaum.

Bennett, J. C. (1990). Nonintervention into siblings' fighting as a catalyst for learned helplessness. *Psychological Reports, 66*, 139–145.

Bohman, M. (1996). Predisposition to criminality: Swedish adoption studies in retrospect. In G. R. Bock & J. A. Goode (eds.), *Genetics of criminal and anti-social behavior,* Ciba Foundation Symposium 194 (pp. 99–114). Chichester, England, and New York: Wiley.

Boney-McCoy, S., & Finkelhor, D. (1995). Psychosocial sequelae of violent victimization in a national youth sample. *Journal of Consulting and Clinical Psychology, 63*, 726–736.

Borduin, C. M., Cone, L. T., Barton, J. M., Henggeler, S. W., Rucci, B. R., Blaske, D. M., & Williams, R. A. (1995). Multi-systemic treatment of serious juvenile offenders: Long-term prevention of criminality and violence. *Journal of Consulting and Clinical Psychology, 63*, 569–578.

197

Bugental, D. B., Blue, J. B., & Cruzcosa, M. (1989). Perceived control over caregiving outcomes: Implications for child abuse. *Developmental Psychology, 25,* 532–539.

Bugental, D. B., Blue, J. B., Cortez, V., Fleck, K., Kopeikin, H., Lewis, J., & Lyon, J. (1993). Social cognitions as organizers of autonomic and affective responses to social challenge. *Journal of Personality and Social Psychology, 64,* 94–103.

Bugental, D. B., Lyon, J. E., Krantz, J., & Cortez, V. (1997). Who's the boss? Accessibility of dominance ideation among individuals with low perceptions of interpersonal power. *Journal of Personality and Social Psychology, 72,* 1297–1309.

Burla-Galili, T. (2001). Sibling abuse and distress of siblings in families characterized by parental helplessness. M.A. thesis, Department of Psychology, Tel Aviv University (in Hebrew).

Cadoret, R. J., Cain, C. A., & Crowe, R. R. (1983). Evidence for gene-environment interaction in the development of adolescent anti-social behavior. *Behavior Genetics, 13,* 301–310.

Caffaro, J. V., & Conn-Caffaro, A. (1998). *Sibling abuse trauma.* New York: Haworth Press.

Cairns, R. B., Santoyo, C. V., & Holly, K. A. (1994). Aggressive escalation: Toward a developmental analysis. In M. Potegal & J. F. Knutson (eds.), *The dynamics of aggression: Biological and social processes in dyads and groups* (pp. 227–253). Hillsdale, N.J.: Lawrence Erlbaum.

Chamberlain, P., & Patterson, G. R. (1995). Discipline and child compliance in parenting. In M. H. Bornstein (ed.), *Handbook of parenting* (vol. 1, pp. 205–225). Mahwah, N.J.: Lawrence Erlbaum.

Clarke, R. V. (ed.) (1992). *Situational crime prevention: Successful case studies.* New York: Harrow & Heston.

Cotrell, B. (2001). *Parent abuse: The abuse of parents by their teenage children.* Ottawa: Family Violence Prevention Unit, Health Issues Division, Health Canada.

Craig, W., & Pepler, D. (1997). Observations of bullying and victimization in the schoolyard. *Canadian Journal of School Psychology, 2,* 41–60.

Dadds, M. R., & Powell, M. B. (1991). The relationship of interparental conflict and global marital adjustment to aggression, anxiety, and maturity in aggressive and nonclinic children. *Journal of Abnormal Child Development, 19,* 553–567.

DeJong, A. (1989). Sexual interactions among siblings: Experimentation or exploitation. *Child Abuse and Neglect, 13,* 271–279.

de Waal, F. B. M. (1993). Reconciliation among primates: A review of empirical evidence and unresolved issues. In W. A. Mason & S. P. Mendoza (eds.), *Primate social conflict* (pp. 111–144). State University of New York Press.

de Young, M. (1982). *The sexual victimization of children.* London: McFarland.

Dishion, T. J., & Patterson, G. R. (1992). Age effects in parent-training outcome. *Behavior Therapy, 23,* 719–729.

Dornbusch, S., Carlsmith, J., Bushwall, S., Ritter, P., Leiderman, H., Hastorf, A., & Gross, R. (1985). Single parents, extended households, and the control of adolescents. *Child Development, 56,* 326–341.

Downey, G., & Coyne, J. C. (1990). Children of depressed parents: An integrative review. *Psychological Bulletin, 108,* 50–76.

Durrant, M., & Kowalski, K. (1990). Overcoming the effects of sexual abuse: Developing a self-perception of competence. In M. Durrant & C. White (eds.), *Ideas for therapy with sexual abuse.* Adelaide: Dulwich Centre.

Eisenberg, N., & Murphy, B. (1995). Parenting and children's moral development. In M. H. Bornstein (ed.), *Handbook of parenting* (vol. 1, pp. 227–256). Mahwah, N.J.: Lawrence Erlbaum.

Farrington, D. P., & West, D. J. (1971). A comparison between early delinquents and young agressives. *British Journal of Criminology, 11,* 341–358.

Finkelhor, D. (1980). Sex among siblings: A survey on prevalence, variety, and effects. *Archives of Sexual Behavior, 7,* 171–194.

Finkelhor, D. (1995). The victimization of children: A developmental perspective. *American Journal of Ortopsychiatry, 63,* 177–193.

Finkelhor, D., & Dziuba-Leatherman, J. (1994). Victimization of children. *American Psychologist, 49,* 173–183.

Florsheim, P., Tolan, P., & Gorman-Smith, D. (1998). Family relationships, parenting practices, the availability of male family members, and the behavior of inner-city boys in single-mother and two-parent families. *Child Development, 69,* 1437–1447.

Frick, P. J., Lahey, B. B., Loeber, R., Stouthamer-Loeber, M., Christ, M. G., & Hanson, K. (1992). Familial risk factors to oppositional defiant disorder and conduct disorder: Parental psychopathology and maternal parenting. *Journal of Consulting and Clinical Psychology, 60,* 49–55.

Funk, W. (1996). Familien- und Haushaltskontext als Determinanten der Gewalt an Schulen. Ergebnisse der Nürnberger Schüller Studie 1994. *Zeitschrift für Familienforschung, 1,* 5–45.

Ge, X., Conger, R. D., Cadoret, R. J., Neiderhiser, J. M., Yates, W., Troughton, E., & Stewart, M. A. (1996). The developmental interface between nature and nurture: A mutual influence model of child anti-social behavior and parent behaviors. *Developmental Psychology, 32,* 574–589.

Geva, R. (1992). *Strategies for crime prevention.* Ministry of Internal Security. Jerusalem, Israel (in Hebrew).

Goldstein, A. P. (1996). *The psychology of vandalism.* New York: Plenum.

Goldstein, A. P., & Conoley, J. C. (eds.) (1997). *School violence intervention.* New York: Guilford.

Gottman, J. M. (1998). Psychology and the study of marital processes. *Annual Review of Psychology, 49,* 169–197.

Gottman, J. M., & Levenson, R. W. (1998). What predicts change in marital interaction over time? *Family Process, 38,* 143–158.

Gully, K. J., Dengerink, H. A., Pepping, M., & Bergstrom, D. (1981). Research note: Sibling contribution to violent behavior. *Journal of Marriage and the Family, 43,* 333–337.

Henggeler, S. W. (1991). Multidimensional causal models of delinquent behavior. In R. Cohen & A. Siegel (eds.), *Context and development* (pp. 211–231). Hillsdale, N.J.: Lawrence Erlbaum.

Hetherington, M., Cox, M., & Cox, R. (1975). Beyond father absence: Conceptualization of effects of divorce. Paper read at the Conference on Social Research and Child Development, Denver, Colo.

Hetherington, E. M., Clingempeel, W. G., Anderson, E. R., Deal, J. E., Hagan, M. S., et al. (1992). Coping with marital transitions: A family systems perspective. *Monographs of Social Research and Child Development, 57,* Ser. No. 227.

Jouriles, E. N., Murphy, C. M., Farris, A. M., Smith, D. A., Richlers, J. E., & Waters, E. (1991). Marital adjustment, parental disagreements about child rearing and behavior problems in boys: Increasing the specificity of the marital assessment. *Child Development, 2,* 1424–1433.

Katznelson, I. (2001). The teacher's figure in public debate. M.A. thesis, Department of Psychology, Tel Aviv University (in Hebrew).

Kenigswald, I. (2001). The authority of adults in the community. M.A. thesis, Department of Psychology, Tel Aviv University (in Hebrew).

Kolko, D., Kazdin, A., & Day, B. (1996). Children's perspectives in the assessment of family violence: Psychometric characteristics and comparison to parent reports. *Child Maltreatment, 1,* 156–167.

Kolvin, I., Miller, F. J. W., Fleeting, M., & Kolvin, P. A. (1988). Social and parenting factors affecting criminal offence rates: Findings from the Newcastle Thousand Family Study (1947–1980). *British Journal of Psychiatry, 152,* 80–90.

Laub, J. H., & Sampson, R. J. (1988). Unraveling families and delinquency: A reanalysis of the Gluecks' data. *Criminology, 26,* 355–379.

Laviola, M. (1992). Effects of older brother-younger sister incest: A study of the dynamics of 17 cases. *Child Abuse and Neglect, 16,* 409–421.

Levenson, R. W., & Gottman, J. M. (1983). Marital interaction: Physiological linkage and affective exchange. *Journal of Personality and Social Psychology, 45,* 587–597.

Levenson, R. W., & Gottman, J. M. (1985). Physiological and affective predictors of change in relationship satisfaction. *Journal of Personality and Social Psychology, 49,* 85–94.

Loeber, R., & Dishion, T. J. (1984). Boys who fight at home and in school: Family conditions influencing cross-setting consistency. *Journal of Consulting and Clinical Psychology, 52,* 759–768.

Loeber, R., & Hay, D. (1997). Key issues in the development of aggression and violence from childhood to early adulthood. *Annual Review of Psychology, 48,* 371–410.

Loeber, R., & Stouthamer-Loeber, M. (1986). Family factors as correlates and predictors of juvenile conduct problems and delinquency. In M. Tonry & N. Morris (eds.), *Crime and justice: An annual review of research* (vol. 7, pp. 129–149). Chicago: University of Chicago Press.

Loeber, R., Weissman, W., & Reid, J. B. (1983). Family interactions of assaultive adolescents, stealers and nondelinquents. *Journal of Abnormal Child Psycholgy, 11,* 1–14.

Matheny, A. P., Jr. (1991). Children's unintentional injuries and gender: Differentiation by environmental and psychosocial aspects. *Children's Environment Quarterly, 8,* 51–61.

Mayer, R. G., Butterworth, T., Nafpaktitis, M., & Sulzer-Azaroff, B. (1983). Preventing school vandalism and improving discipline: A three-year study. *Journal of Applied Behavior Analysis, 16*, 355–369.

McCord, J. (1986). Instigation and insulation: How families affect anti-social aggression. In D. Olweus, J. Block, & M. Radke-Yarrow (eds.), *Development of anti-social and prosocial behavior: Research, theories, and issues* (pp. 343–384). Orlando, Fla.: Academic.

Moffit, T. E. (1990). The neuropsychology of delinquency: A critical review of theory and research. In N. Morris & M. Tonry (eds.), *Crime and justice* (vol. 12, pp. 99–169). Chicago: University of Chicago Press.

Moffit, T. E. (1993). Adolescence-limited and life-course-persistent anti-social behavior: A developmental taxonomy. *Psychological Review, 100*, 674–701.

Moffit, T. E., & Henry, B. (1991). Neuropsychological studies of juvenile delinquencey and violence: A review. In J. Milner (ed.), *The neuropsychology of aggression* (pp. 67–91). Norwell, Mass.: Kluwer Academic.

Neiderhiser, J. M., Reiss, D., Hetherington, E. M., & Plomin, R. (1999). Relationships between parenting and adolescent adjustment over time: Genetic and enviornmental contributions. *Developmental Psychology, 35*, 680–692.

O'Brien, M. (1991). Taking sibling incest seriously. In M. Patton (ed.), *Understanding family sexual abuse.* Newbury Park, Calif.: Sage.

O'Connor, T. G., Deater-Deckard, K., Fulker, D., Rutter, M., & Plomin, R. (1998). Genotype-environment correlations in late childhood and early adolescence: Anti-social behavioral problems and coercive parenting. *Developmental Psychology, 34*, 970–981.

Olweus, D. (1980). Familial and temperamental determinants of aggressive behavior in adolescent boys: A causal analysis. *Developmental Psychology, 16*, 644–660.

Olweus, D. (1993). *Bullying at school: What we know and what we can do.* Oxford, England, and Cambridge, Mass.: Blackwell.

Omer, H. (2000). *Parental presence: Reclaiming a leadership role in bringing up our children.* Phoenix, Ariz.: Zeig, Tucker.

Omer, H., & Alon, N. (forthcoming). The demonic and tragic narratives in psychotherapy and personal relations. In A. Lieblich & R. Josselson (eds.), *Healing Plots: The Narrative Basis of Psychotherapy.* Washington, D.C.: APA Books.

Omer, H., & Elitzur, A. (2001). What would you say to the person on the roof? A suicide-prevention text. *Suicide and Life-Threatening Behavior, 31*, 129–139.

Omer, S. (2001). Restoring the teacher's authority. M.A. thesis, Department of Psychology, Tel Aviv University (in Hebrew).

On, L. (2001). Restoring the teacher's authority in kindergarten. M.A. thesis, Department of Psychology, Tel Aviv University (in Hebrew).

Orford, J. (1986). The rules of interpersonal complementarity: Does hostility beget hostility and dominance, submission? *Psychological Review, 93*, 365–377.

Patterson, G. R. (1980). Mothers: The unacknowledged victims. *Monograph of the Society for Research in Child Development, 186*, vol. 45, no. 5, pp. 1–47.

Patterson, G. R. (1982). *A social learning approach,* vol. 3: *Coercive family process.* Eugene, Ore.: Castalia.

Patterson, G. R., & Capaldi, D. M. (1991). Anti-social parents: Unskilled and vulnerable. In P. A. Cowan & E. M. Hetherington (eds.), *Family transitions* (pp. 195–218). Hillsdale, N.J.: Lawrence Erlbaum.

Patterson, G. R., Dishion, T. J., & Bank, L. (1984). Family interaction: A process model of deviancy training. *Aggressive Behavior, 10*, 253–267.

Patterson, G.R., Dishion, T. J., & Chamberlain, P. (1993). Outcomes and methodological issues relating to treatment of antisocial children. In T. R. Giles (ed.), *Effective psychotherapy: A handbook of comparative research* (pp. 43–88). New York: Plenum.

Patterson, G. R., Reid, J. B., & Dishion, T. J. (1992). *Antisocial boys*. Eugene, Ore.: Castalia.

Perlman, M., & Ross, H. S. (1997). The benefits of parent intervention in children's disputes: An examination of concurrent changes in children's fighting styles. *Child Development, 64*, 690–700.

Plomin, R., Chipuer, H. M., & Loehlin, J. C. (1990a). Behavior genetics and personality. In I. A. Pervin (ed.), *Handbook of personality theory and research* (pp. 225–243). New York: Guilford.

Plomin, R., Nitz, K., & Rowe, D. C. (1990b). Behavioral genetics and aggressive behavior in childhood. In M. Lewis & S. M. Miller (eds.), *Handbook of developmental psychopathology* (pp. 119–133). New York: Plenum.

Potegal, M., & Davidson, R. J. (1997). Young children's post tantrum affiliation with their parents. *Aggressive Behavior, 23*, 329–341.

Ratzke, R., & Cierpka, M. (1999). Der familiäre Kontext von Kindern, die aggressive Verhaltensweisen zeigen. In M. Cierpka (ed.), *Kinder mit aggressivem Verhalten* (pp. 25–60). Göttingen: Hogrefe.

Rausch, K., & Knutson, J. (1991). The self-report of personal punitive childhood experiences and those of siblings. *Child Abuse and Neglect, 15*, 29–36.

Rigby, K., & See, P. (1992). Bullying among Australian school children: Reported behavior and attitudes towards victims. *Journal of School Psychology, 131*, 615–627.

Rothbart, M. K., & Bates, J. E. (1998). Temperament. In W. Damon (series ed.) & N. Eisenberg (vol. ed.), *Handbook of child psychology*, vol. 3: *Social, emotional, and personality development*, 5th ed. (pp. 105–176). New York: Wiley.

Rothbart, M. K., Posner, M. I., & Rosicky, J. (1994). Orienting in normal and pathological development. *Development and Psychopathology, 6*, 635–652.

Salmivalli, C. (1999). Bullying as a group process: An adaptation of the participant role approach. *Aggressive Behavior, 25*, 97–111.

Salmivalli, C., Lagerspetz, K. M., Bjuorkqvist, K., Osterman, K., & Kaukiain, A. (1996). Bulying as a group process: Participant roles and their relations to social status within the class. *Aggressive Behavior, 22*, 1–15.

Schweitzer, J. (1987). *Therapie dissozialer Jugendlicher*. Weinheim: Juventa.

Schweitzer, J. (1997). Systemische Beratung bei Dissozialität, Delinquenz und Gewalt. *Praxis der Kinderpsychologie und Kinderpsychiatrie, 46*, 215–227.

Sharp, G. (1960). *Gandhi wields the weapon of moral power*. Ahmedabab: Navajivan.

Sharp, G. (1973). *The politics of nonviolent action*. Boston, Mass.: Extending Horizons.

Shneidman, E. S. (1985). *Definition of suicide*. Northvale, N.J.: Jason Aronson.

Smith, H., & Israel, E. (1987). Sibling incest: A study of the dynamics of 25 cases. *Child Abuse and Neglect, 11*, 101–108.

Smith, P. K., Morita, Y., Junger-Tas, J., Olweus, D., Catalano, R., & Slee, P. (eds.) (1999). *The nature of school bullying: A cross-national perspective*. London: Routledge.

Spanos, N. P. (1994). *Psychological Bulletin, 116*, 143–165.

Steinberg, L. (1986). Latchkey children and susceptibility to peer-pressure: An ecological analysis. *Developmental Psychology, 22*, 433–439.

Steinberg, L. (1987). Single parents, stepparents, and the susceptibility of adolescents to anti-social peer pressure. *Child Development, 58*, 269–275.

Steinmetz, S. K. (1977). The use of force for resolving family conflict: The training ground for abuse. *Family Coordinator, 26*, 19–26.

Steinmetz, S. K. (1978). Sibling violence. In J. M. Eskelaan & S. N. Katz (eds.), *Family violence: An international and interdisciplinary study*. Toronto: Butterworths.

Straus, M. R., & Gelles, R. J. (1990). *Physical violence in American families: Risk factors and adaptations to violence in 8,145 families*. New Brunswick, N.J.: Transaction.

Thomas, A., & Chess, S. (1977). *Temperament and development*. New York: Brunner/Mazel.

Uziel, K. (2001). Parents, teachers and what goes between them. M.A. thesis, Department of Psychology, Tel Aviv University (in Hebrew).

Wahler, R. G., & Dumas, J. E. (1986). Maintenance factors in coercive mother-child interactions: The compliance and predictability hypothesis. *Journal of Applied Behavior Analysis 13*, 207–219.

Wahler, R. G., & Sansbury, L. E. (1990). The monitoring skills of troubled mothers: Their problems in defining child deviance. *Journal of Abnormal Child Psychology, 18*, 577–589.

Wiehe, V. R. (1997). *Sibling abuse: Hidden physical, emotional, and sexual trauma*. Thousand Oaks, Calif.: Sage.

Wilson, H. (1987). Parental supervision re-examined. *British Journal of Criminology, 27*, 215–301.

Wolfe, D. A. (1987). *Child abuse: Implications for child development and psychopathology*. Newbury Park, Calif.: Sage.

Wood, D. (1991). In defense of indefensible space. In P. J. Brantingham & P. L. Brantingham (eds.), *Environmental criminology*. Newbury Park, Calif.: Sage.

INDEX

abortion, 152
absences, 143, 170
abuse, 5, 86
accusations, 44
activists, 5; act and power of protests by, 172; feelings of self-worth, 36; restraints in, 172
activity, level of, 100
ADD. *See* attention-deficit disorder
addresses, collection of, 29
adjustment, 24
adolescents, 8; dominance orientation, 31; independent identities, 38; reconciliation gestures, 42; response to polarization and cut-offs, 39
adopted children, 102
adoptive parents, 102
adult camps, 181
adult-children polarity, 174, 180–181
adult-free areas, 186, 187
adult violence, 94
aggressive behavior in children, 1; biological factors, 99; and control of households, 125; delinquent behaviors, 47; demands, 27; and escalation, 49; goals in, 4; hereditary factors, 99; individual psychotherapy in treatment of, 75; influence of teachers on, 156; inside classrooms, 187; and lack of systemic parental presence, 98; and

mental disorder, 17; and parliament of the mind, 15; provoking parents, 9; restraining, 28; and sabotage of parental authority, 150; as symptoms of psychological problems, 75
aggressors, identification with, 8
alarm systems, 181
alcohol parties, 171, 174, 176–177
Amsterdam, 177
anarchists, 88
anger, 50
animal behavior, 36
announcement of nonviolent resistance, 50–52; content of, 51; form and timing of, 51; format of, 52
anonymous complaints boxes, 184
antigraffiti paint, 181
antisocial behavior in children, 77; and nonviolent resistance, 48; in single-parent households, 97
anxieties, 99, 143
apes, reconciliation gestures in, 41
apologies, 37
arbitrary punishments, 5
aristocracy, 17
association, 61, 62
asymmetry of means, 9
attacks by children, 50
attention-deficit disorder (ADD), 28; case study, 78; and nonviolent